The Social Roots of American Politics

The Social Roots of American Politics

A Widening Gyre?

REGINA L. WAGNER
and
BYRON E. SHAFER

OXFORD
UNIVERSITY PRESS

Oxford University Press is a department of the University of Oxford. It furthers
the University's objective of excellence in research, scholarship, and education
by publishing worldwide. Oxford is a registered trade mark of Oxford University
Press in the UK and certain other countries.

Published in the United States of America by Oxford University Press
198 Madison Avenue, New York, NY 10016, United States of America.

© Oxford University Press 2022

All rights reserved. No part of this publication may be reproduced, stored in
a retrieval system, or transmitted, in any form or by any means, without the
prior permission in writing of Oxford University Press, or as expressly permitted
by law, by license, or under terms agreed with the appropriate reproduction
rights organization. Inquiries concerning reproduction outside the scope of the
above should be sent to the Rights Department, Oxford University Press, at the
address above.

You must not circulate this work in any other form
and you must impose this same condition on any acquirer.

Library of Congress Cataloging-in-Publication Data
Names: Wagner, Regina L., 1983– author. | Shafer, Byron E., author.
Title: The social roots of American politics : a widening gyre? /
Regina L. Wagner, Byron E. Shafer.
Description: New York, NY : Oxford University Press, [2022] |
Includes bibliographical references and index.
Identifiers: LCCN 2022018860 (print) | LCCN 2022018861 (ebook) |
ISBN 9780197650844 (hardback) | ISBN 9780197650851 (paperback) |
ISBN 9780197650875 (epub)
Subjects: LCSH: Political culture—United States. | Political sociology—United States. |
Political parties—United States. | United States—Politics and government—20th century.
Classification: LCC JK1726 .W24 2022 (print) | LCC JK1726 (ebook) |
DDC 320.973—dc23/eng/20220729
LC record available at https://lccn.loc.gov/2022018860
LC ebook record available at https://lccn.loc.gov/2022018861

DOI: 10.1093/oso/9780197650844.001.0001

1 3 5 7 9 8 6 4 2

Paperback printed by Lakeside Book Company, United States of America
Hardback printed by Bridgeport National Bindery, Inc., United States of America

Turning and turning in the widening gyre
The falcon cannot hear the falconer;
Things fall apart; the centre cannot hold;
Mere anarchy is loosed upon the world,
The blood-dimmed tide is loosed, and everywhere
The ceremony of innocence is drowned;
The best lack all conviction, while the worst
Are full of passionate intensity
                    —William Butler Yeats, "The Second Coming"

CONTENTS

Introduction—The Roots of Political Conflict: Social Cleavages, Policy Preferences, and Partisan Alignments 1

1. The Instantiation of Partisan Alignments: Social Class and Social Welfare 9

2. Enfranchisement and Partisan Alignment: Civil Rights and Racial Background 39

3. Partisan Mobilization and Policy Alignment: Cultural Values and Religious Denominations 65

4. Sex and the Great Reversal in Partisan Alignment: Men, Women, and Policy Preferences 89

Conclusion—The Social Evolution of Postwar Politics: Partisan Alignments since the Second World War 111

Afterword: Partisan Alignments, Voter Priorities, and Presidential Ballots 137
Appendix: Data and Measures 153
Notes 161
Index 173

Introduction

The Roots of Political Conflict

Social Cleavages, Policy Preferences, and Partisan Alignments

How do public wishes become policy conflicts? The usual route to an answer begins with specific conflicts, then works backward. Governmental institutions, as they grapple with those conflicts, are often the starting point. Their actions (or inactions) will, after all, produce the policy outcomes that actually occur. Political parties mounting election campaigns to secure public office are ordinarily the next stop. They make the clearest and most recurrent attempts to mobilize, amend, or straddle policy conflicts on the way to a governmental response. And back behind them, the last links in this causal chain are usually interest groups, issue activists, and mass media. They are the organizational actors who propel more targeted and more specialized wishes for policy outcomes, the grist for what will become conflicts among parties and then within government.

None of that need be false. Yet the whole explanatory chain begins by assuming a critical set of background factors, factors that collectively outweigh these concrete and specific influences. Most fundamentally, the usual version of an explanatory chain assumes the social roots of public support for one or another policy. It goes on to assume the process by which policy preferences arise from and become instantiated in their social roots. Worse yet, it assumes the dynamic by which the policy preferences associated with social cleavages become attached to political parties. We propose to begin at the other end of the causal chain, with an explicit focus on social cleavages, policy preferences, and party attachments. So for us, the lead questions become: how *do* the major social cleavages get translated into policy preferences, and how *does* this opening link get transmitted to political parties and translated into ongoing substantive conflicts?

The Social Roots of American Politics. Regina L. Wagner and Byron E. Shafer, Oxford University Press.
© Oxford University Press 2022. DOI: 10.1093/oso/9780197650844.003.0001

THE SOCIAL ROOTS OF AMERICAN POLITICS

The critical tool for putting all this back together while giving it a concrete embodiment that can be measured is *partisan alignment*. This is the summary device linking social cleavages to policy preferences and converting the link into ongoing conflicts by way of political parties. Pursuit of these alignments requires highlighting the main cleavages in American society. It requires isolation of the policy domains that have been central to modern American politics. It requires distinguishing between those who do the actual work of the parties versus those who vote on the programmatic result but otherwise take a more passive role. More often than not, it requires a side look at the great geographic regions, to be sure that a putatively national story is more than an artifact of differing regional alignments. Finally, the whole enterprise requires a period of time sufficient to allow these "deep factors" to play out (and thereby reveal) their role, while unpacking the change engines that drive this evolution over time.

Social Cleavages, Policy Preferences, and Party Attachments

Accordingly, the remainder of this preface must introduce all these moving pieces, just as it must introduce the generic alignments to which they contribute. It is the composition and character of these alignments that can then be used to track political change in the postwar United States. Such an introduction must begin with the societal bedrock for the entire analysis, in the great social cleavages characterizing American society. Four of these have received continuing attention from scholars concerned with the backdrop to politics, namely class, race, religion, and sex.[1] The need here is to have constant and continuing measures for each of these four cleavages across the last sixty years.

Social class, the seedbed of modern party politics, will be assessed by way of income terciles, yielding upper, middle, and lower classes that can be carried across time. Racial background, defined through the diagnostic categories of the immediate postwar years, namely black and nonblack, is likewise available throughout. The major religious denominations, gathered into four denominational families—Mainstream Protestants, Evangelical Protestants, Catholics, and Others—can, with minimal manipulation, be extended all the way back to the beginnings of the dataset. And sex, last of the four and in some ways the easiest to assemble, can distinguish men from women in all the surveys at work here.

A reading of political history since the Second World War suggests that there have been four great substantive domains for policy conflict since that benchmark event, namely social welfare, civil rights, national security, and cultural values.[2] By the end of the war, American politics had been substantively reorganized by the New Deal, the comprehensive policy effort intended to deal with the Great Depression. The result was an American welfare state, and economic welfare would prove to be both enduring and influential as a policy concern. The second great policy conflict of the postwar period, involving national security, was likewise already in place for the long run, if only citizens of the time had known. Breaking with long historical precedent, the United States would not retreat from international engagements at war's end but instead be a major architect of the postwar international order, which intermittently but insistently injected foreign affairs into domestic politics.

Neither depression nor world war necessarily entailed the rise of the third recurrent conflict of postwar politics, namely civil rights. Yet the 1950s and 1960s would see the emergence of this domain on both electoral and policy agendas, courtesy of widespread social protest, sweeping court decisions, and major legislative enactments, giving it a lasting role in partisan alignments. Finally, the fourth recurring domain in postwar politics was in many ways invisible—more or less dormant—at the end of the Second World War. Yet that meant only that cultural values, far more central to American politics in earlier periods, would see the most striking rise of the four as a source of policy conflict and associated partisan alignments, on occasion surpassing each and all of the other three.

The dominant institutional device for connecting social cleavages to policy domains, intellectually but also practically, is the political party, here in its Democratic and Republican incarnations. So the analysis needs to recognize party attachment, and for this, the canonical measure is long-running and familiar, involving self-identification as a Democrat or a Republican.[3] To capture the dynamics of the partisan alignments central to our main theoretical concerns, however, we shall need to distinguish further by key structural elements—the operational pieces—inside these parties. The ability of political parties to organize partisan alignments will rise across the postwar period, ultimately in every substantive domain. But party plays a shadow role even when this ability is minimal: the irrelevance of party is often a central explanation for the character of the alignments that appear in its absence.

In the process and most centrally, this effort requires a dataset capturing group membership, policy preference, and party attachment. One capable of meeting these demands across time was generated originally for quite other purposes by William Claggett and Byron Shafer, subsequently extended and managed by Regina Wagner.[4] Derived from the American National Election Study (ANES), its measures were a product of comprehensive exploratory and then confirmatory factor analyses, yielding scales for public preferences on social welfare, national security, civil rights, and cultural values. In what follows, the results are presented as standard scores—standardized but not normalized—with negative numbers representing liberal preferences, those left of the national average, and positive numbers representing conservative preferences, those right of that average.

Lastly, the years since the Second World War—though these are really the years since the first round of what would become the ANES in 1952—are able to provide the necessary time span, a stretch sufficient to allow the interaction of all these elements in a fashion that is not idiosyncratic to particular elections. In order to study change over time while retaining statistical reliability during an extended postwar era, these years are aggregated into three periods with five elections each: hence an opening period, 1950–1970; a second, successor period, 1970–1990; and a third period, effectively our modern world, 1990–2010.

In principle, those measures allow the systematic presentation of policy preferences for four major substantive domains in three elementary but revealing ways. The first involves the stratification of public preferences by party attachment. Party not only is the most common and straightforward of aligning principles in everything that follows but also will remain the most instructive means of comparison even when it is not the dominant organizing influence. The second instead features the stratification of public preferences by social cleavage. As an aligning device, social cleavages can trump party attachment; they can shape policy alignments *inside* the parties; or they can be entirely subsumed by them. As a result, the third means of stratifying policy preferences merges these two organizing principles, as cleavages within parties, for a focus on the joint impact of their organizing influence on partisan alignment.

All three fundamental means of shaping policy alignments can be presented as a national portrait by calculating the ideological position of parties, cleavages, or the two jointly through data for the nation as a whole. Yet regional divisions have long been a staple in the interpretation of American politics, and they were much in evidence at the beginning of the postwar era.[5] Within a welter of regional possibilities, the great and indisputable division in the United States was North versus South. So an analysis of the evolution of partisan alignments needs to check continually on the degree to which national portraits are truly nationwide, being roughly replicated in the major regions; recognizable within each of these regions but anchored and shaped differently by factors specific to one or the other; or a mechanical average of regional differences, adding up to nothing that should rightfully be called "national."

Among further influences shaping partisan alignments, the last major addition is internal party structure, that is, stratification by levels of participation inside political parties. The two key levels distinguish party activists, those who do the actual work of the party, by comparison to the rank and file, who identify with the party and come out to vote, ordinarily for its candidates, but who are not otherwise active in intraparty politics. The ANES has long carried a small battery of items that ask about specialized political activities, and these allow us to make this distinction, one that creates a final, four-part divide: activist Democrats, rank-and-file Democrats, rank-and-file Republicans, and activist Republicans.[6] These partisan populations not only provide a snapshot of internal party politics at a particular point in time but also offer a window on the way in which partisan pieces were shifting in their policy preferences, a crucial aspect of political change more generally.

That is an introduction to the social cleavages, policy conflicts, and party attachments that will contribute to partisan alignments in the chapters that follow, shaped from the outside by geographic regions that compete with political parties for aligning influence, and shaped from the inside by party structures that transmit while they further shape the resulting alignments. In the end, it is these partisan alignments that become the crucial "moving pieces" for interpreting the evolution of political conflict across the postwar years, so tracking their evolution becomes the critical means of isolating and explaining overall change in the structure of American politics. The central focus, however, remains the process by which basic social cleavages become linked to policy preferences, links that are then pulled into political parties, where party actors translate them into policy conflicts and transmit these conflicts into government.

Along the way, each of the conventional major cleavages gives rise to a different major engine of change, change engines that, while having serious spillover impacts, derive most diagnostically from specific social cleavages and particular policy domains. From social welfare and social class, the critical change engine is a largely implicit process of instantiation, persistence, and extension. From racial background and civil rights, the central engine is instead a formal process of voter enfranchisement, altering the very definition of the political community while more or less requiring a subsequent chain of mutual adjustments among its members. From religious denomination and cultural values comes a conscious strategic process, partisan mobilization, whereby latent values are activated by rising policy conflicts that are then picked up and driven by political parties. From sex and national security, finally, though this proves to be almost a different *kind* of linkage, a social cleavage generates its main political influence more directly, by altering individual party attachments and overall partisan balance.

Chapter Outlines

What remains for an introduction is to set out the chapter outlines for all of that, with special attention to the central themes energizing individual chapters. Chapter 1 begins with the great instantiating alignment of the postwar party system. This is the alignment that grew up around social welfare. Its key underlying cleavage was social class. And they were already linked by party attachment as the postwar era began. In that sense, a partisan alignment emerged fully instantiated by the end of the Second World War. Yet this initial instantiation would prove sufficient to facilitate the integration of new social situations with new policy initiatives as they arose, so that the original alignment would only grow across all the years to come. Other policy domains would achieve a roughly parallel alignment over time. Yet the original incarnation of this particular nexus between class, policy, and party would make the partisan alignment on social welfare into a comparative template for all the others, while remaining sufficient to keep social welfare itself at the center of American politics.

Chapter 2 turns to the alignment contributing the deepest policy divide of these postwar years. The critical cleavage here was racial background. The diagnostic policy domain was civil rights. And the link between the two would undergird a veritable civil rights revolution, whose critical product for an analysis of partisan alignments would be the formal (re)enfranchisement of black Americans. When it arrived as a change engine, on a scale sufficient to alter the racial balance of the American electorate, voter enfranchisement would set off a further chain of mutual adjustments among its various contributory pieces. The rights domain would also be the first to come into an alignment roughly parallel to the one characterizing social welfare, though racial background would remain distinctive from social class as a supporting cleavage and interact with party attachment in a manner different from all other policy realms.

Chapter 3 shifts to partisan mobilization as a change engine, whereby latent policy preferences become attached to emergent policy conflicts that are then actively harnessed by the political parties, acquiring a manifest impact on partisan alignments in the process. The key social cleavage was religious denomination. The lead policy domain was cultural values. And the resulting alignment, very unlike those on social welfare and civil rights, was one that had to be consciously recognized, fostered, and pursued. The main religious denominations never really altered their policy preferences. Rather, what changed was a rising partisan divide inside these denominations, where a link between religious groups and cultural issues was deliberately forged from the interaction of changes in the larger society and changes in the policy postures of the active parties. That said, differential impacts by religious denomination would be further fueled by sharply different patterns of denominational growth and decline.

Chapter 4 turns to a change in partisan alignments of a different sort. The key social cleavage here was sex, but there was to be no single policy domain that consistently distinguished men from women. So one part of what distinguished sex from the other cleavages was the continuing fluidity of the policy differences associated with this division. Yet the larger part of what distinguished sex—and

Introduction

the real change engine here—was a direct and growing link between sex and party identification, expanding across the postwar period and shifting the party balance for the nation as a whole as it did so. At the beginning of the postwar era, men were slightly more Democratic than women. By the end, men were clearly more Republican. Yet for a cleavage that was always split roughly fifty-fifty, Democratic gains among women were not offset by Republican gains among men. Rather, net change augmented the Republican Party and diminished its Democratic opposition.

The Conclusion turns to three major collective themes for partisan alignments across the postwar years, then closes with a synthesizing return to everything that came before. The first of these collective themes involves the gradual but ineluctable convergence of partisan alignments across four major policy domains. The second returns to these four stories with a focus on the rise of party attachment and the decline of geographic region within converging alignments. And the third collective theme turns back to the evolution of major social cleavages within those evolving alignments, where, unlike region, these cleavages retain their distinctive roles within what are nevertheless increasingly shared alignments. A return to the evolutionary stories of four separate domains by policy content then completes the chapter.

Most of the electoral impact of these partisan alignments—and more of it as time passed—can be traced back to partisan alignments, that is, to the diagnostic links among social cleavages, policy preferences, and party attachments. In that sense, any time a Democrat votes Democratic or a Republican votes Republican, the necessary explanation has already been produced. There is little further to be learned; the vast bulk of the result is intrinsic to prior partisan alignments. The exceptions lie among those who did *not* vote in accord with their chosen parties. So the Afterword attends to issue priorities among these dissident voters. Seen this way, social welfare dominates the opening period. It is joined by a further contribution from national security in the successor era. And the modern world shifts to a dual emphasis on a constantly influential social welfare and explosively rising cultural values.

In the end, there is a picture of changing policy conflicts across the postwar period, one developed from systematic data, broken down by policy preference, social cleavage, and party attachment, then reassembled into partisan alignments. This picture encompasses the great realms for policy conflict, namely social welfare, civil rights, national security, and cultural values. It encompasses the social cleavages that give rise to preferences within those realms, namely social class, racial background, religious denomination, and sex. It situates the link between policy preferences and social cleavages in the nature of their attachment to political parties, the attachment that is largely responsible for converting those links into institutionalized and ongoing political conflicts. In the process, it highlights four major change engines, namely instantiation, enfranchisement, mobilization, and conversion.

On one level, the result is careful delineation of those partisan alignments across the postwar period, ideally with enough detail to allow the component parts to have recognizable impacts of their own, but impacts that are not simply a product of some larger—unexamined—background context. More abstractly, this result is simultaneously an attempt to get beyond the inherently distortive approach to telling that same story by way of one domain, one cleavage, or one time period, then extrapolating—almost always inaccurately—to larger generalizations that are usually the partial product of something else. If the result also reaches back to some fundamental questions about where policy conflicts come from, and if it offers a framework for taking those questions forward, applying them at other—especially future—points in time, then it will have contributed what it aspires to contribute.

‖ 1 ‖

The Instantiation
of Partisan Alignments

Social Class and Social Welfare

The traditional starting point in a search for the social roots of partisan alignment is social class, and the conventional policy domain for registering class
preferences is social welfare. Yet in the years immediately following the Second
World War, this was far more than just an analytic expectation based on tradition
and convention. The central narrative of American politics in the decade before
the war had involved the Great Depression, the New Deal as a policy response to
it, and public attitudes toward the coming of an American welfare state. A world
war had put all that on hold, but the war was over. So the unresolved questions
for the opening years of the postwar period revolved around social welfare, social class, and the link between them, along with the manner and the degree
through which this link was instantiated by the two major parties.

In principle, the New Deal might have proven to be an earth-shaking policy
response to a cataclysmic but transient crisis, with political conflict either set-
tling back into the patterns characterizing American politics before these concentrated initiatives or moving on to what this politics would become when the
Great Depression and the New Deal were no longer central concerns.[1] In practice, however, the immediate postwar years were to confirm the place of social
class as the dominant cleavage in American politics. In the process, it was social
welfare that was institutionalized by the two great opposing parties, social welfare that continued to be the policy core of this "New Deal party system," and in
fact social welfare that would polarize additionally through all the years to come,
helping to drive the two parties farther apart while helping to restructure individual attachments inside them.

Or at least, this analysis aspires to demonstrate that those are the facts,
not all of which are taken to be consensual. At the extreme, there are analysts

The Social Roots of American Politics. Regina L. Wagner and Byron E. Shafer, Oxford University Press.
© Oxford University Press 2022. DOI: 10.1093/oso/9780197650844.003.0002

who believe that the earliest years in this chronicle should more accurately be gathered as "the first New Deal," perhaps coupled with a modest but expansive "second New Deal" but distinguishing both from normal politics. This is an implicit argument that the welfare domain waned early as a policy focus. In a more indirect demurral, there are analysts who believe that because other concerns would rise as continuing matters of policy conflict—foreign affairs, civil rights, and cultural values most especially—the place of social welfare would gradually but inevitably erode. It would not disappear; economics and welfare policy were too important for that to happen. But the domain would increasingly have to share policy impact with those others, and the process of jostling for influence would reduce the centrality of welfare policy to American politics.[2]

The challenge for those who think not—as we think not—is thus more or less automatic and comes in three parts, which become the organizing principles for Chapter 1. First, did the expected link between social class and social welfare return to the center of American politics, allowing the political parties to instantiate this link through partisan alignments that demarcate the postwar world? Second and by contrast, what happened to the obvious challenger to political parties as an organizing principle for public preferences and policy conflict, namely geographic region? Region was, after all, a long-established and still-intrusive alternative for shaping policy alignments. Third and regardless of either preceding answer, how did the partisan alignment connecting social class and social welfare to political parties evolve? Was it rising but also falling on its own terms? And did it maintain centrality or was it pushed aside by links between other social cleavages and other policy domains?

A Partisan Instantiation for Welfare Preferences

The opening version of what was to become the American National Election Study (ANES) arrived in 1952, well after both the Great Depression and the New Deal response to it had run their course. The ANES was thereafter to provide the most comprehensive, consistent, and continuous body of survey evidence for tracking partisan alignments.[3] It likewise remains at the center of everything that follows here, and it explains why our version of the postwar world begins in 1952. The narrative of the time was then otherwise very straightforward with regard to our initial question, about the institutionalizing power of social class and social welfare.

First, public preferences on social welfare were said to have returned as the focus of American politics in the years following the Great Depression and the Second World War. In the process, social class was said to have challenged geographic region as the societal bedrock of welfare preferences. In response, the political parties were said to have moved the welfare state to the center of their policy programs. Lastly, and again reciprocally, rank-and-file Americans were believed to have begun sorting themselves as Democrats or Republicans according to their policy preferences on social welfare. With the benefit of hindsight, aided by sixty years of ANES surveys, we can know that the opening period of the postwar years, defined here as 1950 to 1970, did indeed pass all these tests.

A clear partisan divide on welfare preferences was already present by the time the ANES went into the field, with Democrats to the left of the national average and Republicans to its right (Table 1.1.A). Political parties in other societies may have been more polarized on these concerns, but American parties were clearly distinguished by welfare preferences as this first postwar period arrived.[4] With standardized scores and a two-category variable—Democrats versus Republicans—the absolute distance of the two parties from the national average cannot otherwise be compared: more adherents meant a comparatively lower score for the larger party, the Democrats, and a comparatively higher score for the smaller party, the Republicans. Yet the scale of overall alignment on social welfare, that is, the ideological distance between the two parties, was already impressive. None of the other possibilities for a similar policy role—civil rights, national security, or cultural values—came close.

In truth, the narrative of the time was composed of two connected pieces. The first involved this division of policy preferences on social welfare by party attachment, captured here in Table 1.1.A. The second was an assumption that this policy division was rooted in preferences deriving from social class. In theory, the poorest parts of American society, being hardest hit by the Great Depression, seemed naturally biased toward welfare responses. The richest parts of this same society, being better buffered against the same stresses, seemed naturally biased away. In practice, the Democratic Party was thought to have reorganized

Table 1.1 **Party Attachment, Social Class, and Policy Preference: Social Welfare, 1950–1970**

A. By Party		B. By Class	
Dems	−.17	Low	−.11
Reps	+.24	Mid	−.05
		High	+.12

C. By Classes within Parties					
Democrats			*Republicans*		
Low	*Mid*	*High*	*Low*	*Mid*	*High*
−.24	−.18	−.09	+.11	+.15	+.39

its policy program to reflect economic values and class conflict. The Republican Party might have preferred an entirely different focus, yet it had little choice but to respond, though different state parties would make different choices as between conscious adaptation and stubborn resistance.[5]

Table 1.1.B suggests that this second part of the generalization too was supported by survey research. While there were Democrats and Republicans, liberals and conservatives, in every social class (about which, more below), lower-income Americans were collectively if modestly liberal on welfare policy, upper-income Americans were collectively if modestly conservative, and middle-income Americans fell more or less naturally in between. That said, there was a further aspect to this relationship that was also important to the politics of the time. To wit: this relationship was not symmetric, with the three classes proportionately spaced out by policy preference. Rather, there was an implicit class coalition, pitting low-income plus middle-income Americans against their upper-income fellow citizens.

In principle, one or the other of these overarching associations—policy positions aligned by party attachment or policy positions aligned by social class—could have dominated the combined relationship, to the point where the other link was rendered spurious. Table 1.1.C confirms, however, that this was not the case. Both party attachment and class membership were aligned with welfare preferences even in the presence of the other. Moreover, the resulting composite was not just aligned by parties but neatly ordered by classes within them. The most liberal Americans were low-income Democrats, the most conservative were high-income Republicans, and every other mix of party and class assumed its ideologically appropriate position in between.

Inside that array, even high-income Democrats were liberal—party attachment did not lose its impact even for them—though this was only a modest liberalism. And even low-income Republicans were conservative, though this in turn was a modest conservatism. That said, the truly outlying population was upper-income Republicans, standing distinctively off from the national average. As if to underline that fact, both low-income and middle-income Republicans were actually closer to high-income Democrats than to their upper-income co-partisans. Indeed, the scale of this division inside the Republican Party—low and middle classes against the upper class—was largely what explained the class coalition that appeared to characterize society as a whole in Table 1.1.B.

Yet by the time of the first ANES survey in 1952, there was a second policy domain that was widely perceived to be central to political conflict in American society. This was foreign affairs, with a special focus on national security.[6] Moreover, during that first ANES survey, the United States was engaged not in a cold but in a very hot war on the Korean Peninsula, as it would be engaged in another such venture, in Vietnam this time, during the last survey of this

Table 1.2 Party Attachment, Social Class, and Policy Preference: National Security, 1950–1970

A. By Party		B. By Class	
Dems	−.02	Low	−.01
Reps	+.02	Mid	+.03
		High	−.02

period. Accordingly, the hypothesis that this other domain with its continuing national attention would also achieve some form of partisan alignment was not unreasonable—not unreasonable, as it turns out, but clearly wrong. Table 1.2 confirms the absence of any such alignment, or even a hint thereof.

Aggregated by party attachment, the two parties showed nearly no difference in policy desires by their respective identifiers on national security (Table 1.2.A). Both the Democratic and the Republican Parties sat very close to the national average, rendering the two parties ten times as polarized on social welfare as they were on national security. With hindsight, at least two explanations for this lack of alignment present themselves. In one, the two parties as they came out of the Great Depression were cross-cut by approaches to national security, with each possessing serious isolationist and internationalist wings. In the other, though not inconsistently, the nation had been overwhelmingly united in pursuit of World War II and remained essentially united in the face of the Cold War, a unity sufficient to make obvious dissidence by either party look strategically unwise.[7]

Whatever the mix of explanations, party attachment clearly did not organize noteworthy divisions in the policy domain of national security. Moreover, social class likewise introduced no divisions that would have imparted an alternative structure to this second policy domain. Like the two major parties, the three classes were effectively indistinguishable in their security preferences (Table 1.2.B). All three sat nearly on the national average, and even the tiny differences among them did not assume any ideologically linear order. Accordingly, of the two great policy domains widely believed to be central to policy conflict in this first postwar period, social welfare had already achieved a clear and systematic alignment, by party attachment and by social class, while national security had yet to achieve either, much less both.

Yet that is still an incomplete approach to the resulting partisan alignments on social welfare, because it assumes the same level of engagement with politics for every survey respondent. A more realistic way to visualize the policy alignment of the welfare domain in this opening period, and especially to unpack its implications for practical politics, is to distinguish additionally between

14 THE SOCIAL ROOTS OF AMERICAN POLITICS

those who did the actual work of the two political parties—in effect, the active party—and those who confined their political activity to responding to what the active parties put before them, effectively their rank and file.[8] Table 1.3 does just that, and the picture of partisan conflict that emerges is both more complex and more realistic as a result.

The Democratic and Republican rank and files (DRF and RRF), further stratified by class membership, confirm a basic class difference between the parties (Table 1.3.A). Voter turnout still inherently skews the class base of both, consistently diminishing the bottom tercile and consistently augmenting the top. Yet within this differential sampling, Democrats and Republicans remained socially different. The Democratic Party was close to being a rough sample of the class distribution for the nation as a whole, with a modest bonus to upper-class Democrats. But the Republican Party skewed clearly toward upper-class identifiers, who came very close to being a majority of the party as it surfaced at the polls. Finally, what resulted for the two rank and files together was a party system characterized by obvious but not dramatic class differences.[9]

Very different was the class composition of the two active parties (DAc and RAc), not so much by comparison to each other but rather by comparison to their own rank and files. This second intraparty difference, likewise coming into view when the parties are stratified by level of political activity, showed both active parties sampling the class base of their rank and files in a strong but parallel fashion: activists were far more likely than their rank and file to be upper-class individuals, among Democrats and not just Republicans. Moreover, this difference was not only large on both sides of the partisan aisle but also slightly larger among Democrats than among Republicans. Said differently, the class

Table 1.3 **Partisan Populations and Social Classes, 1950–1970**

A. Class Contributions to Partisan Populations

	Low	*Mid*	*High*
DAcs	20%	26%	54%
DRFs	34%	30%	36%
RRFs	25%	30%	45%
RAcs	16%	19%	65%

B. Class Contributions to Activist Preferences

	DAc	*DRF*	*RRF*	*RAc*
Actual Preferences	−.19	−.17	+.20	+.39
Adjusted Preferences	−.23	−.17	+.20	+.34

distributions among party activists on both sides of the partisan aisle were closer to each other than either one was to its own nominal rank and file.

But how much did this matter? The question of what these activists would have looked like if they had been a more accurate class sample must be treated with caution. Subsequent analyses for all four partisan populations in all four policy domains will confirm that the four populations were capable of making autonomous moves in their ideological positioning. Even in this opening period, the ideological gap between upper-class identifiers in the two parties was larger than the counterpart gap between party identifiers in either of the other two classes. Yet one simple data-based means for generating policy alternatives for both sets of activists does not require a deliberate change by anyone, while it provides a measure of the share of policy preferences within the active parties that trace from class membership independent of party attachment.

For this, it is not difficult (and requires no further manipulation) to retain the policy preferences that actually characterized each of the three social classes inside two activist populations, but to ask what these preferences would have added up to in the aggregate if they had been calculated on the class composition that characterized their respective rank and files, rather than on the distribution that actually characterized the active parties. Table 1.3.B does this, first presenting the welfare preferences held by all four partisan populations, then contrasting them with the preferences that would have been generated among party activists if they had possessed the same class composition as their rank and files. Results are unsurprising and modest but clear.

When the two rank and files are presented this way, in the absence of their activists, party attachment remains a strong influence. Democrats are still clearly to the left and Republicans clearly to the right, though the two do look increasingly symmetric without their activists. So the organizing power of party attachment in the aggregate is hardly an artifact of activist preferences. When the two active parties are allowed back into this picture, two further things stand out. First, both sets of activists stood farther from the national average than their respective rank and files. But second, this representational gap was small among Democrats, where the rank and file and their activists were closely clustered, though this relationship would change significantly in subsequent eras.[10] Yet the same difference—the representational gap between party activists and their own rank—was much larger among Republicans, making Republican activists the true ideological outliers on social welfare.

What happens if we then allow all these activists to retain their actual preferences but mix them according to the class composition of their rank and file? The second line of Table 1.3.B offers an answer. As they were distributed by class in the political world of the time, Democratic activists stood at −.19 on social welfare, very close to their rank and file. When reshuffled to reflect the class distribution of their rank and file, they move to −.23, opening an additional policy gap with this rank and file though still not a huge one. Conversely, as they were actually distributed by social class, Republican activists stood at +.39, almost twice as conservative as their rank and file. When reshuffled to reflect the class distribution of this rank and file, they move to +.34, reducing the gap while still leaving it twice as large as its Democratic counterpart.

So the most basic point is still that the composite alignment of welfare preferences by partisan population in this opening period retains its underlying form quite apart from differential class sampling. Party rank and files were ideologically distinct in their welfare preferences, while party activists flanked them to the left for Democrats and the right for Republicans. What the over-representation of the upper class among these activists contributed was to pull each activist population measurably but modestly to the right on social welfare, simultaneously making the underlying alignment less ideologically symmetric than it would have been had these activists been a more accurate sample of the class distribution of their respective rank and files, while making Republican activists look additionally conservative.

Regional Impacts on Partisan Alignment

Yet even at the time, there was a third major alternative for organizing policy preferences, for social welfare or indeed for any other domain. For social welfare, the first was party attachment, and the second was social class. Each brought an ideological alignment to welfare preferences, and each exercised its influence in a partially autonomous fashion. Neither made the other superfluous, while both were driving in the same direction. But all that said, there was a third grand alternative, one with a long reach across American history and an obvious—and vigorous—presence in the politics of the day. This third organizing principle was geographic region, and in the United States of the time, that meant first and foremost a long-running and often deep division between the North and the South.

Over time, a great deal of intellectual coherence could be imparted to American politics by viewing it through this regional lens.[11] So it seems essential to return to the national alignment and ask whether it constituted a truly general portrait, realized a bit differently in specific locales of course, but generalized in its essentials, or whether, at the other extreme, the national portrait was little more than a mechanical composite of regional portraits, whose serious differences were obscured by a national picture that was in effect a statistical artifact, purporting to show an overarching pattern that did not exist anywhere

Social Class and Social Welfare

Table 1.4 **Party Attachment, Social Class, and Policy Preference: Social Welfare by Geographic Region, 1950–1970**

	A. By Party		B. By Class			
	Dems	*Reps*	*Low*	*Mid*	*High*	
North	−.21	+.24	−.10	−.06	+.09	North
South	−.05	+.25	−.12	−.06	+.25	South

C. By Classes within Parties

	Dems			*Reps*			
	Low	*Mid*	*High*	*Low*	*Mid*	*High*	
North	−.27	−.22	−.17	+.13	+.16	+.35	North
South	−.19	−.07	+.14	+.11	−.01	+.46	South

in application (Table 1.4). To that end, Table 1.4 repeats the original picture of welfare alignments by party attachment, social class, and classes within parties, divided this time into two great political regions.

A return to welfare preferences by region as well as party shows immediate and major differences from the national picture (at Table 1.1.A). Perhaps surprisingly, however, what appears initially is not two versions of a shared alignment, colored by regional differences. Instead, what appears are two separate alignments, specific not to geographic regions but to the individual parties (Table 1.4.A). Seen this way, the Republicans appear as a truly national party from the start, unaffected by region, with a Southern component that was indistinguishable on the surface from its Northern counterpart. Conversely, the Democrats appear as a regional party first and foremost, with a Northern component anchored in far more liberal territory than its Southern counterpart, which was sitting only modestly left of the national average.

A further focus on regional party *systems* makes this initial difference look eminently reasonable, that is, structural rather than idiosyncratic.[12] In particular, one aspect of a party system that is often taken to be foundational, namely the degree of competitive balance between its individual parties, leads quickly to a major regional twist on welfare alignments. Classified by party balance, the North featured a clear but narrow Democratic majority, the defining mark of a competitive party system.[13] This was accompanied by two Northern parties that were well apart in their welfare preferences, in a modestly stronger but more symmetric fashion than the national picture suggested. So this non-Southern portrait of party attachment and policy preference was more or less the stereotypical outcome of a closely competitive party system.

By contrast, the South had long been essentially a one-party region, where Democrats still outnumbered Republicans by three to one as the postwar period began.[14] Ironically, it was this very imbalance that made Southern Republicans appear to be much like Northern Republicans, while simultaneously driving a wedge between Southern Democrats and their Northern counterparts. For Southern Republicans, this competitive imbalance had produced a minority party with little more than a skeletal structure, kept alive by a leadership existing largely to funnel federal patronage back to their states. A party this small and this dependent on external contributions had no incentive to differ from—and potentially alienate—Northern colleagues on welfare preferences, a result that fits neatly with the fortunes of the minority party in an uncompetitive party system.[15]

Yet for Democrats, the same imbalance meant that a sizable share of the population that would have been Republican elsewhere was perforce Democratic in the South, the Democratic Party being the only route to public office or, for that matter, to policy influence.[16] It is impossible to know how many Southerners were Democrats on such purely pragmatic grounds, but however many there were, they had to be a conservatizing influence on the Southern Democratic Party. At the same time, there was a major missing liberal influence. Black Americans still resided disproportionately in the South, where they were the social group that was also disproportionately disfranchised. Once championed by Southern Republicans, black Southerners had become solidly Democratic where they could actually vote, as well as overwhelmingly liberal on social welfare, making them the missing liberal influence on the Southern Democracy.[17]

Class comparisons by region—welfare preferences by social class, North versus South—are the essential next step in understanding the operation of these regionally distinctive party systems (Table 1.4.B). Yet even more than with policy alignments by party attachment, alignments by social class present a focused rather than a general impact by region. Welfare preferences among the lower classes actually did not differ between the regions. Neither, for that matter, did welfare preferences among the middle classes. But welfare preferences in the upper classes were hugely divergent. Wealthy Southerners were so far to the right even of wealthy Northerners that the entire class spectrum in the North, from lower to upper classes, was no greater than the distance between just the Northern and Southern upper classes.

This made regional divisions inside an upper class the key to a Southern exceptionalism in the immediate postwar years.[18] And that was another large regional distinction that had to be pursued through consideration of the shaping influence of party and class jointly, though region could still add critical distinctions to this interaction (Table 1.4.C). Seen this way, the North largely recapitulated the joint alignment evident for the nation as a whole, one running neatly by steps from low-income Democrats to high-income Republicans. Yet the South jumbled this alignment dramatically. Nothing was linear in the Northern (and national) fashion. Instead, the left on welfare preferences was contributed by low-income and middle-come Democrats. The center was contributed by low-income and middle-income Republicans. And the right was contributed by upper-income Republicans and upper-income *Democrats*.

Seen the other way around, by classes across regions rather than by regions across classes, the ideological distance between upper-income Democrats in the North and upper-income Democrats in the South was by far the largest such policy difference, the one that stood out in a combined consideration by party, class, and region. By comparison, the ideological distance between upper-income Republicans in the North and upper-income Republicans in the South was unimpressive.[19] Yet to see the ultimate practical impact of those combined impacts, it is necessary to break out the regional alignments not once but twice, first for the four partisan populations, then by social classes within those populations.

When this is done, the rank and files themselves look notably different as between the two regions, though what this difference really reflects is the grinding poverty of the South in these early postwar years (Table 1.5.A). The

Table 1.5 **Partisan Populations and Social Classes by Region, 1950–1970**

A. Class Contributions to Partisan Populations

	1. North			2. South			
	Low	Mid	High	Low	Mid	High	
DAcs	19%	26%	55%	21%	27%	52%	DAcs
DRFs	31%	31%	38%	42%	29%	29%	DRFs
RRFs	29%	29%	42%	42%	26%	32%	RRFs
RAcs	13%	19%	68%	31%	20%	49%	RAcs

B. Class Contributions to Activist Preferences

1. North

	DAc	DRF	RRF	RAc
Actual Preferences	−.25	−.21	+.21	+.39
Adjusted Preferences	−.28	−.21	+.21	+.31

2. South

	DAc	DRF	RRF	RAc
Actual Preferences	+.02	−.06	+.14	+.49
Adjusted Preferences	−.16	−.06	+.14	+.39

much larger share of Southern society that was still in subsistence agriculture means that both parties had a larger lower class, in the South than in the North, coupled with a smaller upper class. Beyond that, Northern Democrats were much more evenly divided by class, while Southern Democrats were clearly weighted toward the lower class, even in the absence of black Southerners and even in the presence of electoral rules that discriminated against poorer nonblack Southerners. Northern Republicans likewise looked much like the national picture of a class distribution for their party, while the same extensive Southern poverty actually made low-income Republicans the modal class within their regional party.

For the nation as a whole, party activists then told a quite separate class story, one shared across the two parties while again distinguished from their own rank and files. By region this time, both activist populations strongly overrepresented their upper-income identifiers, at the expense of both middle- and lower-income fellow partisans. And again, the more striking fact was that the resulting class distributions for party activists were closer to each other—much closer—than either was to their own rank and file. This was true in the North, where the representational difference by social class was large among Democrats and larger among Republicans. And it was true in the South, where the gap was likewise large among Republicans and Democrats.

So once again, the insistent question becomes how much the differential sampling of social classes by the active parties mattered to the policy preferences they presented. Half an answer is simple (Table 1.5.B.1). In the North, with Southerners absent from the sample, the recalculated Democratic activists looked slightly more liberal than they had for the nation as a whole, while Republican activists, more strongly affected by internal class sampling, looked considerably more liberal with their Southern counterparts removed from the picture. Together, what would have resulted was an ideological alignment of Northern partisan populations that was nearly symmetric. Class sampling pulled the entire alignment only modestly to the right, though the outlier status of Republican activists was much more directly a product of differential class sampling.

Yet the other half of an answer to the question of the policy impact from class sampling, and massively the larger half, came in the South, in a story that had to be told in two parts (Table 1.5.B.2). In the lone point of interest within a still-skeletal Southern Republican Party, though this too was in essence a class story, the Southern rank and file was actually less conservative than the Northern rank and file among Republicans, a difference that looked only more striking because Republican activists stood so far to the right on social welfare in the South, right of their Northern counterparts but also twice as far from their own rank and file by comparison to the North. Southern Republican activists, as scarce as they were in these opening postwar years, sustained—and presumably were sustained by—a welfare conservatism well right of everyone else.

Southern Democrats, however, were the far larger part of this regional story, both in the nation as a whole and within its Democratic Party. When the two parties were treated as national aggregates, the Democrats looked solidly liberal in the North (at −.21) and only marginally liberal in the South (at −.05). But now, further stratified by partisan population, it is Southern Democratic activists who jump off the page, being dissident on social welfare in every regard. They were ever so marginally conservative, and not liberal at all. They were the partisan population farthest from their Northern counterpart, the Northern Democratic activists. And they were actually right, not left, of their own putative rank and file. Indeed, this latter fact was sufficient to give the South a partisan alignment in the welfare domain that was different *in kind* from the Northern version.

In the North (and the nation), the left-to-right ordering on welfare preferences ran from Democratic activists to the Democratic rank and file to the Republican rank and file to Republican activists. But in the South, it ran from the Democratic rank and file to Democratic activists, before repeating the usual alignment among Republicans. So it was not that the two parties merely differed in the ideological placement of their welfare preferences by region, with the South more conservative. The South was actually more liberal among rank-and-file Republicans. But among Democrats, geographic region gave the South a partisan alignment that was different in kind from its Northern counterpart, with Democrats right of center nationwide, and well right of their own rank and file. Yet there was more. In fact, Southern Democratic activists were the lone partisan population where a differential sampling of the class distribution among their rank and file was more important than regional differences themselves in shaping the policy preferences of these dissident activists.

In the real political world (the first line of Table 1.5.B.2), these activists were modestly right of the national average (at +.02). But had they retained the same preferences by class but been an accurate sample of the class distribution among the Southern Democratic rank and file, they would have been clearly liberal (at −.16) and not conservative at all (as in the second line of Table 1.5.B.2). Moreover, had this been the case, the entire welfare alignment for Southern partisan populations would have assumed the same form as its Northern counterpart, just anchored in more conservative territory. Lastly, Southern Republican activists would have been more strongly moderated than their Northern counterparts by an accurate class sample, though still clearly at the conservative end of the ideological continuum. This means that class sampling among party activists was uniformly more consequential in the South than in the North, and extremely consequential among Southern Democrats.

The Evolution of a National Alignment

The partisan alignment generated from the link between social class and welfare policy, as institutionalized by party attachment, was to appear unshakable as time passed. Indeed, the aligning power of party attachment would only expand—not just stabilize, much less decline—across all the years after the opening postwar period[20] (Table 1.6). The three other major policy domains would evolve toward a roughly parallel ultimate alignment, but less neatly, starting weaker and moving more idiosyncratically. Yet the links from social cleavage to policy preference to party attachment for social welfare would make this the most clearly aligned domain at the beginning of the postwar world, while its evolving alignment would make it the standard for comparing developments in the three other domains over time.

Different periods would bring different specific embodiments of welfare policy to the fore: unemployment insurance, old-age pensions, health care, child care, food support, disaster relief, and on and on.[21] Yet none of these would diminish, or even recast, the aligning character of the welfare domain as originally instantiated. Table 1.6.A confirms the continuation of this power across both successor periods. In the opening years, there was already a serious ideological distance between self-identified Democrats and self-identified Republicans, dwarfing counterpart distances in the three other domains. Yet partisan divergence on social welfare was to become larger, not smaller, in the successor era,

Table 1.6 **Party Attachment, Social Class, and Policy Preference: Social Welfare across the Postwar Period**

	A. By Party		*B. By Class*			
	Dems	*Reps*	*Low*	*Mid*	*High*	
Era 3	−.24	+.36	−.17	+.02	+.16	Era 3
Era 2	−.24	+.26	−.22	+.01	+.14	Era 2
Era 1	−.17	+.24	−.11	−.05	+.12	Era 1

C. By Classes within Parties

	1. Dems			*2. Reps*			
	Low	*Mid*	*High*	*Low*	*Mid*	*High*	
Era 3	−.31	−.23	−.17	+.16	+.38	+.44	Era 3
Era 2	−.39	−.20	−.11	+.10	+.25	+.34	Era 2
Era 1	−.24	−.18	−.09	+.11	+.15	+.38	Era 1

and that growing distinction would only continue to expand in the most recent period.

Still, if the ideological divide between the two parties on welfare policy was institutionalized, predictable, and increasing, it was just as clearly not growing in a linear fashion for individual parties, much less from any strategic response by one to the other, and least of all in some bipartisan fashion encompassing both. Rather, one or the other of the major parties would disproportionately impel the ideological polarization that characterized each of the periods to follow. The big jump from the first to the second occurred among Democrats, with little movement among Republicans, though this Democratic move will prove (in the following section) to owe a great deal to regional developments. Yet the big jump in the third period was even more clearly located among Republicans, with hardly any action from the Democrats, and this Republican move would prove truly national.

In turn, nothing about the evolution of the link between class membership and welfare preferences, the one at the social root of these other relationships, would threaten this institutionalized and growing role for social welfare as a policy domain. Rather, the class cleavage too would expand over time, though as with party attachment, each individual class was to follow its own path[22] (Table 1.6.B). The upper class proved the most linear and most stable, shifting modestly to the right in its welfare preferences in each succeeding period. The middle class was to chart a truly middling course, in which the original class coalition pitting the lower and middle classes against the upper class would see the middle class hew more closely to the genuine ideological center, leaving it closer to the upper than the lower class but clearly independent of both.

Lastly, the lower class would move clearly opposite to the upper class across time, augmented by a noteworthy leftward leap in the second period. This leap will look less distinctive when geographic region is brought back into the picture and less idiosyncratic when compared to upper-income Democrats and middle-income Republicans, both of whom made even larger moves within their respective parties. Chapter 2 will root this ideological jump additionally in direct fallout from the instantiating impact of the welfare alignment during the opening postwar years, coupled with a disproportionate one-time increment from voter enfranchisement of black Americans—weighted, as they were, toward the lower end of the class spectrum.

For now, however, the point is that despite an ongoing polarization of welfare preferences among party identifiers, joined to individually wandering paths by the social classes, the combined result—welfare preferences by classes within parties—would prove regular, patterned, and relentless (Table 1.6.C). The opening partisan alignment had been neatly linear, running from lower-class Democrats on the left to upper-class Republicans on the right with every population in its appropriate place in between. Yet the exact same pattern, as challenging as it was to reproduce both in theory and in practice, was to be replicated in the second postwar period, then repeated, again exactly, in the third.

Because there is no way to track the movement of particular individuals within the parties and classes that were jointly generating this recurrent behavior—we cannot know where any survey respondent stood last time—it is not possible to ask whether respondents were individually stable in their welfare preferences inside a remarkably stable collective result. It is, however, easy to ask about the direct relationship between class membership and party attachment. Presumably, given aggregate preferences by class, an increased tendency by the lower class to identify as Democrats or the upper class to identify as Republicans would contribute an additional increment to partisan alignment.[23] Table 1.7 sets up this search, putting the Democratic share first and the Republican share second (D/R) for each social class in each era. Once again, there are three stories to go with the three classes.

Members of the lower class began as heavily Democratic and became only more so as time passed. The increase was not huge, but its direction was clear and consistent. At a minimum, this shift both reflected and reinforced the overall partisan alignment on social welfare. Members of the middle class drifted more than the other classes, tending Republican in the second period while tending back toward Democratic in the third, but always fronting a Democratic majority. The upper class made the biggest partisan shift, looking even bigger because it took the group all the way from a Democratic to a Republican majority. In the opening period, even this upper class leaned Democratic, though by the smallest margin of the three. Yet the group swung Republican, solidly, in the second period and remained there for the third. This too both reflected and reinforced an overall partisan alignment on social welfare.

The remaining element that contributed to shaping the national alignments stemming from social class, welfare preferences, and party attachment was the internal structure of the parties themselves, as captured most especially by the distinction between party activists and their rank and files. In the opening postwar period, this further distinction made the two rank and files, absent their activists, look slightly less polarized and slightly more symmetric. Among the

Table 1.7 **Party Attachment among Social Classes across the Postwar Period**

	Low	*Mid*	*High*	
Era 3	69/31	59/41	46/54	Era 3
Era 2	64/36	56/44	45/55	Era 2
Era 1	62/38	61/39	54/46	Era 1

Table 1.8 **Policy Preference by Partisan Population: Social Welfare across the Postwar Period**

	DAcs	DRFs	RRFs	RAcs
Era 3	−.32	−.23	+.32	+.53
Era 2	−.31	−.22	+.23	+.36
Era 1	−.19	−.17	+.20	+.39

activists, both flanked their rank and files in the orthodox direction, Democrats to the left and Republicans to the right, though Republican activists were so much farther from the national average than their Democratic counterparts that they qualified as the true outliers in welfare politics.[24]

When this form of analysis is extended across time, it normally offers more scope for policy change among these activists, who tend to be both more policy focused and more willing to take extreme positions than their rank and files (Table 1.8). Still, the rank and files offered one lesser and one substantial policy shift in the years after the opening postwar period. The lesser shift came in the immediate successor era, when the two populations became more symmetric. Both continued to polarize, but the Democratic rank and file moved farther than its Republican counterpart. Yet the major shift came in the modern world, and this time it belonged almost solely to the Republican rank and file, more than canceling that previous move toward symmetry. The Democratic rank and file was nearly stationary in this modern shift, while the Republican rank and file moved strongly to the right.

Yet when party activists move to the center of the analysis, three further results specific to the active parties appear, each larger than these rank-and-file effects. In the first, activists continued to flank their rank and files on the ideological extremes, though as we shall see in later chapters, this ideological placement did not uniformly characterize the other domains. Second, Republican activists continued to be more extreme than Democratic counterparts, by a great deal in the opening period, by comparatively little in the middle period, and by more again in the modern era, though this relationship was often reversed in the other domains. And third, party activists implicitly reminded the analyst that they were capable of autonomous moves, away from their rank and files or even, on occasion, opposite to them, though the rank and file was fully capable of independent shifts as well.[25] The leftward leap by Democratic activists in the second postwar era was one example of this third activist effect. More striking was a modest leftward move among Republican activists in the same period, striking because their rank and file was simultaneously moving in the opposite ideological direction.

26   THE SOCIAL ROOTS OF AMERICAN POLITICS

This brings the analysis back to a fresh version of the final question from the first postwar period: how much of the ideological gap between party activists and their rank and files was due to independent differences in policy preference and how much was due only to differential sampling by social class? The answer in the first era strongly favored genuine differences in policy preference. If the two active parties had been more representative of their rank and files by class, both would have moved leftward, augmenting the liberalism of Democratic activists while moderating the conservatism of Republican counterparts. Yet this Democratic result was small in absolute terms, while the Republican version, albeit larger, was an even smaller contribution to total activist preferences.

Over time, the question becomes, how much of this change in activist positions, and most especially of the changing gap between party activists and their own rank and files, was due to actual shifts in policy preference, and how much was again due simply to differential representation by social class? For the second era, the answer is immediately different as between the parties (Table 1.9.A). This is the period when the aggregate Democratic Party moved strongly leftward, a move that was considerably exaggerated among its activists, who traveled from −.19 in the old world to −.31 in the new. Yet most of this change could still be traced to altered preferences. If these activists had possessed a class distribution similar to that of their rank and file, they would have gone even farther left, from −.31 to −.34. But three-quarters of a major activist change remained a matter of hearts and minds and not of differential sampling.

By contrast, the Republican Party experienced little of either in this second period. Republican activists moderated slightly in the new era, traveling back toward the center, from +.39 to +.36. So overall change was small. If these activists

Table 1.9 **Class Contributions to Activist Positions: The South**

A. Era 2

	DAc	DRF	RRF	RAc
Rescaled by Class	−.34	−.22	+.23	+.35
New Preferences	−.31	−.22	+.23	+.36
Previous Preferences	−.19	−.16	+.20	+.39

B. Era 3

	DAc	DRF	RRF	RAc
Rescaled by Class	−.33	−.23	+.32	+.50
New Preferences	−.32	−.23	+.32	+.53
Previous Preferences	−.31	−.22	+.23	+.36

had possessed a class distribution identical to that of their rank and file, they would have moderated a hair more (to +.35), but all these differences are minimal. Overall change remained worthy of attention here not because of these absolute numbers but because Republican activists were actually moving in a direction opposite to their rank and file, leftward for the activists, rightward for their constituents.

The third period then flipped these modest comparative effects. Democratic activists were nearly immobile between eras, moving from −.31 to −.32, which would have increased to −.33 if class sampling had been more accurate. So if both effects were present, they were also trivial. By comparison, the shift among Republican activists was huge. Abandoning their incipient moderation from the preceding period, these activists leapt off to the right, moving all the way from +.36 to +.53, almost half again as far from the national average as they had previously been. Had these activists better reflected the class distribution of their rank and file, this leap too would have moderated slightly, back from +.53 to + .50. But the overwhelming impact derived from changed preferences and not from differential sampling.

Regional Contributions to an Evolving National Picture

A focus on the evolution of partisan alignments for social welfare by region highlights the second postwar era as the site of one of the biggest changes in all of postwar politics. Concretely, this period saw a huge diminution in the distinctiveness of the Southern Democrats as a regional party. More abstractly, a great regional divide that had characterized American politics for a very long time, certainly from the 1850s through the 1960s, began to close. Geographic region would survive for one more era as an alternative organizing principle for public preferences on civil rights. It would survive into the modern era as a secondary organizer for public preferences on cultural values. Yet for public preferences on social welfare, region as a distinctive aligning influence had disappeared early in this second postwar era.

When the postwar world began, Northern and Southern Republicans already stood in the same ideological place across the regions, while Northern Democrats hewed closely to the national Democratic alignment[26] (Table 1.10.A). So it had been the ideological dissidence of Southern Democrats that underpinned a major regional divide in the welfare domain. Little was to happen in the North during the successor era. Northern Democrats would edge left, becoming ideologically symmetric with Northern Republicans in their policy preferences. But that was really all. Only in the third postwar era did a Northern party make an ideological shift with substantial impact on national alignments, and this would come from

Table 1.10 Geographic Region and Policy Preference: Social Welfare across the Postwar Period

A. By Party

	1. North		2. South		
	Dems	Reps	Dems	Reps	
Era 3	−.24	+.35	−.26	+.36	Era 3
Era 2	−.24	+.25	−.22	+.29	Era 2
Era 1	−.21	+.24	−.05	+.25	Era 1

B. By Class

	1. North			2. South			
	Low	Mid	High	Low	Mid	High	
Era 3	−.15	+.01	+.15	−.19	+.03	+.18	Era 3
Era 2	−.16	−.01	+.10	−.30	−.01	+.23	Era 2
Era 1	−.10	−.06	+.09	−.12	−.06	+.25	Era 1

C. By Classes within Parties

1. North

	Dems			Reps			
	Low	Mid	High	Low	Mid	High	
Era 3	−.31	−.23	−.17	+.13	+.38	+.44	Era 3
Era 2	−.40	−.23	−.14	+.16	+.24	+.29	Era 2
Era 1	−.27	−.22	−.17	+.13	+.16	+.35	Era 1

2. South

	Dems			Reps			
	Low	Mid	High	Low	Mid	High	
Era 3	−.32	−.22	−.19	+.18	+.36	+.44	Era 3
Era 2	−.39	−.15	−.07	−.02	+.24	+.55	Era 2
Era 1	−.19	−.07	+.14	+.11	−.01	+.56	Era 1

Northern Republicans, moving strongly to the right, coming into alignment with their newly muscular Southern contemporaries.[27]

So what had diagnostically disappeared in the second postwar era was the regional gap on welfare preferences inside the national Democratic Party, the one where Northern Democrats sat originally at −.21 and Southern Democrats at

−.05. Northern Democrats did shift modestly leftward, remaining slightly left of their Southern counterparts. But by comparison to the opening era, this difference was inconsequential. The Republican Party would make a major shift to the right in the modern period, and this would be true of both regional Republican parties. By then, the Southern Democrats, moving left again while Northern Democrats remained essentially stationary, had not only closed the policy gap with their Northern counterparts but also became ever so slightly the ideological left on social welfare for the nation as a whole.

The postwar alignment of welfare preferences by social class would begin with another strong regional difference, this one focused on the Northern and Southern upper classes. Yet it too would move toward parallel alignments, of social class by region this time[28] (Table 1.10.B). In the opening period, it was the further dissidence of a Southern upper class—far to the right of every other class cohort, North or South—that really distinguished the regions, over and above party attachment. The successor period was to see this class divide morph into a common alignment, a trifle more exaggerated in the South but otherwise parallel. And the modern world would come close to eliminating regional differences by class, with just a tiny echo of that previously greater Southern polarization.

Though what this particular combination of class membership and party attachment implied for an overall partisan alignment was the critical story for social welfare. In this, the North offered impressive stability across time (Table 1.10.C.1). In the opening period, there was already a neatly ordered ideological continuum running from low-income Democrats on the left to upper-income Republicans on the right, and the same could be said for both the successor era and the modern world. Within this, lower-class Democrats made a major one-time move to the left in the successor era, while upper-class Republicans made a major one-time move to the right in the modern era. But the only class-based partisan group in the North to show regular change was middle-class Republicans, moving strongly rightward in both successor eras.

This is yet another way of saying that crucial change was again concentrated in the South[29] (Table 1.10.C.2). Originally, the Southern region had in effect replaced the national (and Northern) alignment by party and class with one that put low-income and middle-income Democrats on the left, low-income and middle-income Republicans in the center, and upper-income Republicans plus upper-income *Democrats* on the right. Even more than with aggregate differences by party attachment or class membership, it was this joint impact that made the South politically distinctive. This was the dissident alignment that had to disappear in a regional convergence during the second postwar period if the South was to come into national alignment, and stay gone in the third.

As in fact it did. By the modern era, all six Southern cohorts by party and by class essentially fronted the same policy preferences in both the North and the South. Along the way, all traces of the old regional divide on social welfare evaporated. The really big change—the one that ended what was effectively a Southern exceptionalism—had to come among those originally dissident upper-income Southern Democrats, and they were to move all the way across the ideological center in the second era, from conservative to liberal, before extending this new liberalism into the modern world. Yet there was to be a secondary shift within the Southern Republican Party, an ascendant party gaining importance in the second postwar period before assuming regional leadership in the modern era.

The old Southern Republican Party, having been sustained in Appalachia, the poorest part of the old South, had possessed an extreme class divide within its limited social confines. The rank and file had been comparatively moderate on social welfare, a moderation that made the extreme conservatism of upper-income Southern Republicans look additionally striking.[30] Through the long and losing years, these upper-income Republicans had provided the sustenance for a skeletal Republican Party. Yet unlike the Democratic story, which featured upper-income Southern activists rejoining the national party, it would be lower- and middle-income Republicans who joined their activists as the party began to grow, achieving middle-class conservative conformity in the second postwar period and lower-class conservative conformity only in the third.

What was going on here? Some of this change was indirect fallout from larger changes in the policy domain of civil rights, addressed comprehensively in the next chapter. But some of it was a logical product of the institutionalization of a partisan alignment on social welfare during the previous period. By this successor era, policy preferences on social welfare by party and by class had become much more self-evident, and thus harder to escape (Table 1.11). In response, for both the North and the South, the share of partisans who were out of alignment with their party on social welfare fell, differentially by region and by era but declining reliably nevertheless. Two different measures tell this story.

Measured by the share of rank-and-file Democrats who were right of Republican activists or the share of rank-and-file Republicans who were left of Democratic activists, a relatively demanding standard for misalignment, both sets of misaligned populations dropped strikingly over time (Table 1.11.A). In the North, Democratic identifiers had come into alignment earlier, so misaligned Republicans declined more at first, though Democrats would more than catch up in the modern period. In the South—recall that there were three times as many Southern Democrats as Southern Republicans at the start—both misaligned populations fell noticeably in both periods.

Measured instead by the share of rank-and-file Democrats who were right of the Republican rank and file or the share of rank-and-file Republicans who

Social Class and Social Welfare 31

Table 1.11 **Policy Misalignment by Party across the Postwar Period**

		A. With Party Activists		B. With the Rank and File	
		1. North	2. South	1. North	2. South
Era 1					
	Dems	13%	22%	20%	30%
	Reps	26%	28%	27%	39%
Era 2					
	Dems	13%	17%	22%	27%
	Reps	15%	16%	21%	21%
Era 3					
	Dems	4%	6%	11%	14%
	Reps	11%	12%	15%	15%

were left of the Democratic rank and file, a less demanding standard, the percentage of those who were out of alignment with their party was of course larger. In the South, 30% of Democrats and 40% of Republicans were out of line by this measure at the start, a huge ideological jumble left over from the one-party era. So the resulting shift was under way earlier in the South than in the North, though both parties had caught up in both regions by the modern period.[31]

As ever, it was not possible to track the movement of particular individuals within the parties and classes that were jointly generating this result. Still, it remains easy to ask about the direct relationship between class membership and party attachment over time, now as divided into two great regions, and the resulting picture tells three stories (Table 1.12). In the first, the conventional link between party and class is essentially unbothered by splitting it into regional pieces. In the second, regional differences by social class decline clearly across all three eras for the full postwar period. But in the third, the South moves far more than the North in the course of producing these other results.

The now-familiar class relationship turns up everywhere, with the lower class most Democratic, the upper class most Republican, and the middle class in between but leaning Democratic. This was true in all periods and for both regions. Moreover, both regions moved from less polarized to more polarized by social class. Class was only modestly related to party balance in the immediate postwar years, but strongly related by the modern era. That is a change entirely consistent with—presumably driving and being driven by—a rising partisan alignment for policy preferences on social welfare. Yet all that said, the South moved much more strikingly within those common patterns, beginning as clearly less polarized than the North in party attachments by social class but

Table 1.12 Party Attachment among Social Classes: Geographic Regions across the Postwar Period

A. North

	Low		Mid		High		
	Dems	Reps	Dems	Reps	Dems	Reps	
Era 3	64%	36%	61%	39%	48%	52%	Era 3
Era 2	58%	42%	52%	48%	43%	57%	Era 2
Era 1	57%	43%	56%	44%	51%	49%	Era 1

B. South

	Low		Mid		High		
	Dems	Reps	Dems	Reps	Dems	Reps	
Era 3	74%	26%	57%	43%	42%	58%	Era 3
Era 2	75%	25%	64%	36%	51%	49%	Era 2
Era 1	75%	25%	78%	22%	72%	28%	Era 1

ending up clearly more polarized by the modern era. That is, in turn, a change entirely consistent with—again driving and being driven by—the convergence of partisan alignments across regions and across time.[32]

What is left is only to ask about the further shaping impacts on this evolutionary picture when viewed through internal party structure. In the North, that story is simple. The two Democratic populations, that is, the active party plus its rank and file, changed only marginally over the entire postwar period. Both became slightly more liberal, while the activists remained consistently left of their rank and file. So unlike all three of the other major policy domains, as we shall see, a partisan alignment for social welfare among Northern Democrats was effectively in place when the Second World War ended. Democratic activists liberalized in the immediate postwar years, but that was roughly the entire story of change.

The two Northern Republican populations, the active party and its rank and file, told a Republican version of the same story. Stable in their preferences between the first and the second postwar eras, both shared the strong Republican move to the right during the modern era. Otherwise, beginning farther from their rank and file than Democratic activists were from theirs, Republican activists sustained this larger representational gap in the modern period. The result was a collective story of stable partisan alignment, instantiated in the opening period while polarizing across time, with this polarization driven more by Republicans than Democrats as time passed.

Table 1.13 Policy Preference by Partisan Population: Social Welfare across the Postwar Period by Region

A. North

	DAcs	DRFs	RRFs	RAcs	
Era 3	−.32	−.22	+.32	+.53	Era 3
Era 2	−.32	−.23	+.22	+.34	Era 2
Era 1	−.25	−.21	+.21	+.37	Era 1

B. South

	DAcs	DRFs	RRFs	RAcs	
Era 3	−.31	−.25	+.31	+.60	Era 3
Era 2	−.37	−.20	+.29	+.40	Era 2
Era 1	+.02	−.06	+.14	+.49	Era 1

After the opening period, the Southern version was to be much like this Northern story. Before that, however, a serious Southern dissidence, largely among the Democrats, was what had made geographic region a major influence on welfare alignments, second only to party attachment. In the beginning, the South did not even place the four partisan populations in the same ideological order. Instead, both Democratic populations were not just well right of their Northern counterparts; Southern Democratic activists were so additionally conservative as to sit to the right of the national average. Yet this was an old world that would be demolished in the shift toward a common partisan alignment in the second period, to the point where, by the modern era, there would be almost no difference in welfare preferences for any of the four partisan populations, in the South or in the North, apart from a slightly augmented conservatism among Southern Republican activists. Along the way, both Southern Democratic populations moved to the left, so strongly for their activists that they ultimately surpassed their Northern counterparts in welfare liberalism. When these Southern Democrats did that, the old dissident ordering of welfare preferences among partisan populations disappeared from the South. But by the modern period, region would no longer be even a serious secondary influence on partisan alignments for social welfare.

The Instantiation of Social Welfare

In the years immediately following the Second World War, and indisputably by the time there was survey data in a form that could be followed across all the years thereafter, American politics had come to feature a diagnostic partisan alignment. This alignment was rooted in the link between social class and public preferences in the policy domain of social welfare, a link that had already become connected to—instantiated in and carried forward by—party attachment. Moreover, the resulting alignment would remain in place while growing only stronger over the next *sixty years*. American society would change hugely between 1950 and 2010. Yet this alignment would stay at the center of its politics, in a form that could be confirmed through a set of continuing measures. This was the partisan alignment that became the bedrock of the American party system.

That particular outcome was hardly inherent. Before the Great Depression, the New Deal, and the coming of the welfare state, class membership was almost certainly connected to policy preferences in a different fashion, in which geographic region—with regional economies—was every bit as important as party attachment for instantiating this linkage. Systematic opinion surveys were not yet available to specify its details, but a great deal of historical work supports this view of an alternative prior alignment with a very different connection among policy, class, and party.[33] Systematic surveys began to arrive during the 1930s and 1940s, suggesting that the modern alignment, while it could be glimpsed intermittently if the analyst knew where to look, was hardly regularized when the arrival of World War II drove it from the center of American politics.

Yet by the first ANES survey in 1952, an alignment connecting welfare preferences, class membership, and party attachment could be readily seen and then recurrently located, in the fashion that it would still be displaying some sixty years later.[34] There were analysts who believed that this alignment would inevitably fade, growing weaker as the Great Depression disappeared into historical memory. There were analysts who believed that the alignment would instead be muscled out of the way as counterpart alignments came increasingly to the fore. So if all of the analysis in this opening chapter had to be reduced to a single point, it would be that both sets of analysts were rather clearly wrong. Instead, policy preferences on social welfare had become instantiated in party attachment, to the point where they became the comparative template for evolving partisan alignments in other policy domains as well.

Perhaps unsurprisingly, welfare preferences were simultaneously instantiated in class membership, with the lower class liberal, the middle class moderate, and the upper class conservative. Individual classes would vary in their evolution and in the class coalitions among them. Yet for the two relationships applied simultaneously, linking welfare preferences jointly to party attachment and class membership, neither ever subsumed the other. Rather, there was a roughly linear association with policy preferences that was arrayed by both. The most liberal cohort was low-income Democrats, the most conservative was upper-income

Republicans, and every cohort in between fell in the appropriate place, by classes within parties.[35]

All of this was true for the welfare domain, though not, as we shall see, for the three major others. National security in particular can be argued to have been every bit as pressing as social welfare in the years encompassing the end of the Second World War and the beginning of the Cold War. Yet no counterpart alignment in that otherwise rising and portentous policy domain emerged. Public preferences on national security were unrelated to party attachment, unrelated to social class, and unrelated to the combination of the two. Instead, the subgroups derived from both of these potential organizing principles sat more or less equally and uniformly on the national average when the focus is foreign affairs.

Yet if welfare preferences linked to social class were instantiated by party attachment across all these years, the two parties hardly lost the capacity for autonomous initiatives. In the generation after the immediate postwar period, the Democratic Party would shift leftward on social welfare, while the Republican Party stayed close to its previous position. But in the generation after that, the Republican Party would move more sharply off to the right, while the Democratic Party remained essentially static. So major individual moves confirmed the autonomy of the major parties, despite a stable overarching alignment. What they also demonstrated was most definitely *not* some requirement that the two parties respond in parallel ways, even to common developments, much less that they respond to movements by each other. Instead, change in partisan alignments was more likely to come from changing forces inside one or the other of these parties.

Yet all of this—the place of party attachment and the role of social class in jointly organizing public preferences on social welfare—was repeatedly influenced in two additional ways. From the inside, an enduring alignment was further shaped by party structure, most especially the internal division within each party between party activists, those who did the operative work of the party, versus their rank and file, party identifiers whose role was ordinarily limited to voting on programs presented by the active party. From the outside, that enduring partisan alignment was shaped additionally by geographic region. Once, region might actually have displaced party inside this institutionalized alignment. By the beginning of the postwar era, this was no longer true, though region retained sufficient influence to mottle the dominant alignment in important ways.

There were reliable differences between the active party and its rank and file in the other policy domains but not necessarily in the same manner as with social welfare. In the welfare domain, party activists were reliably more extreme than their rank and file, Democrats to the left and Republicans to the right, apart from the major Southern exception referenced later. Because these activists were more extreme, the rank and files looked more moderate and more symmetric in their absence, though social welfare never lost a clear division by party attachment (and social class) even among the rank and file. Beyond that, with social welfare but really in none of the other policy domains, Republican activists were always more ideologically extreme than their Democratic counterparts.

Given those ongoing differences, it should come as no surprise that Republican activists provided the best examples of autonomous ideological moves.[36] In the opening postwar era, these activists stood out for their distance both from the national average and from their own rank and file. In the successor era, Republican activists stood out for the opposite reason, by providing a rare era-to-era moderation by an activist population, where a move back toward the center was additionally striking because their rank and file was moving in the opposite direction. In the modern period, finally, Republican activists regained the spotlight by diving back off to the right, remaining the most extreme partisan population while sitting even farther from the national average, from the other party, and from their own rank and file.

Yet the great activist dissent of the entire postwar period, dwarfing this internal Republican story, belonged to the Southern Democrats in the opening years. So it is their behavior that introduces the overall story of regional dissent, an archetypal story of region trumping party as an influence on policy alignments. The moment party and class are further divided by North versus South, it becomes clear that an initial neat and systematic patterning to partisan alignments in the nation as a whole was in part a statistical artifact. Because the North was the larger geographic region, a national outcome showed up clearly in the North, contributing the larger half of the national story. Yet at the same time, an apparently national alignment did not show up in the South at all, which means that a partisan alignment for the nation as a whole was the mechanical sum of two very different regional alignments.

There were some parallel elements inside even this major regional deviation. Democrats were more liberal and Republicans more conservative, both North and South. The poor were more liberal and the rich more conservative, again both North and South. But at that point, the parallels disintegrate, through a class-based divergence focused pointedly on the Southern upper class. Policy preferences in both the lower and the middle classes were essentially identical by region, while the upper classes went on to contribute the ideological right in both. Yet the difference between the Southern and the Northern upper classes was huge, larger than the difference between the lower and the upper classes for the nation as a whole. Said differently, upper-class Southern Democrats sat not just to the right of Democrats of all classes in the North as well as the South, but to the right of lower- and middle-class Southern Republicans.

The result was an ideological order in the South that was different in kind from that of the North (and the nation), whereby Southern Democratic activists were not even on the left of their region, much less pulling it off to the left, though the ability of upper-class Southern Democrats to alter the fundamental ordering of partisan populations was additionally dependent on a cascading set of representational advantages. Its members were the most active element within the dominant party in a one-party system. They were further advantaged by an oversampling of the upper class among party activists, an oversampling that was exaggerated in the poorest part of the country, the one with the largest lower class. And this cascade was completed by the absence of a large but effectively disfranchised black population, concentrated in the South and tilted toward the low end of the class continuum.

The result was extreme: even if Southern Democratic activists had maintained their same (very conservative) preferences on welfare policy but merely been an accurate sample of the class base of the Southern Democratic Party—quite apart from the distortions inherent in a one-party system and in substantial disfranchisement—they would have been very slightly liberal as a cohort, and the South would have presented only a less liberal version of the national (and Northern) alignment. Instead, the Southern upper class was gifted—or gifted itself—with dissident preferences that acquired exaggerated impacts in both regional and national politics. All of this went a long way toward explaining the pivotal position of Southern Democrats in the national politics of the time.[37]

The power of their leadership cadre was strongly augmented by the fact that they headed the most reliably Democratic part of the nation. Until the postwar period, their support in presidential voting was unfailing, while there were years when they were an actual majority of the Democrats in Congress. This was in turn a clout that could be wielded by what were comparatively misaligned party activists, more able to make policy deals with Northern Republicans than were the Northern Democrats. Among their rank and file, the moderate welfare preferences of the Southern Democracy made them not only the partisan population closest to the national average but also the population most able to tolerate partisan defection by their leadership, when it was inclined to desert Northern Democrats and join Northern Republicans, especially on issues of social welfare.[38]

On the other hand, the Southern Democrats in this first postwar period would also represent the last hurrah of an established regional dissent on social welfare. In the immediate postwar years, they were still a reflection of the old world rather than the new, a world where region trumped party as a means of organizing policy preferences. This was the regional divide that would be swept away in the successor era, through a combination of fallout from the ongoing institutionalization of a postwar policy alignment on social welfare plus reforms aimed at voter enfranchisement. These latter developments will be central to Chapter 2. In the meantime, the major point is different.

When the old Southern regional alignment disappeared in the second postwar period, the displacement of party attachment by geographic region as shaping influences on partisan alignments disappeared as well. In the first era, region was the basis of an alignment that was different in kind from the national picture, simultaneously rendering the composite national version artifactual. For the second era, the role of region would be reduced to locating parallel alignments in distinctly more conservative territory for the South as opposed to the North. Region as the basis of an alignment that was different in kind from this national pattern would be gone. And by the third era, even this secondary impact would disappear. Republican and Democratic partisan populations would be ideologically identical by party, North versus South, and regional influences would no longer be in evidence.

In the end, then, with a view of all three postwar periods, a national picture of partisan alignments on welfare policy can be seen to have been consistent and relentless, so regular as to make continuing comment almost redundant. Democrats were always left of Republicans. The lower class was always left of the middle class, which was always left of the upper class. And a combination of those two organizing principles fueled regular, recurrent, and ideologically linear alignments across classes within parties. This was true in the immediate postwar years, with critical caveats. It would still be true, more extensively and with no caveats, in the modern era. There had been one gigantic exception at the start, in a Southern partisan alignment privileging region over party. But when that disappeared in the succeeding era, the old national pattern became clearly dominant, then stronger and stronger. What remained was a template—in effect, a measure—by which to compare the evolution of other policy domains and other social cleavages.

2

Enfranchisement and
Partisan Alignment

Civil Rights and Racial Background

The partisan alignment gathering social welfare and social class was noteworthy for having arrived by the time of the inaugural American National Election Study (ANES) survey. Yet this alignment would remain noteworthy for the organizing potential that it was to sustain thereafter, easily outdoing the stability of its three main competitors: civil rights and racial background, cultural values and religious denomination, and national security and sex. Those characteristics hardly meant that the welfare alignment itself did not evolve over time. But they did mean that the engine of change for the link among welfare, class, and party remained the strength of its initial instantiation, coupled with the way this linkage could be constantly refreshed by new policy concerns that operated in the same basic manner.

The absence of a policy domain or social cleavage with comparable influence in the opening postwar years hardly ruled out the rise of other domains and different cleavages as time passed. Nor did the rough stability of welfare preferences and class membership mean that new policy conflicts and new social divisions would inevitably mirror them, either in the manner by which they arrived or in the trajectory by which they evolved. Indeed, there are *multiple* generic engines of change in American (or almost any) politics. We shall attend to three of these in the chapters that follow:

- Rising policy conflicts can become attached to previously dormant social cleavages, then be mobilized by political parties, altering partisan alignments in the process. That is the grand story of cultural values and religious denomination.

The Social Roots of American Politics. Regina L. Wagner and Byron E. Shafer, Oxford University Press.
© Oxford University Press 2022. DOI: 10.1093/oso/9780197650844.003.0003

- Established cleavages can instead shift their policy connections, and thus their partisan implications, as society translates old substantive connections into new policy concerns with a different aligning potential. That is the grand story of national security and sex.
- Yet what is in some sense the most basic engine of change involves the formal contours of the political community itself, that is, conscious changes to the aggregate of those who get to constitute the partisan alignments of any given time. That is the story of civil rights and racial background, the substance of Chapter 2.

On one level, change in the composition of the electorate is ineluctable and relentless. Yet it is also so glacial that it often disappears from view without the ability to interrogate an extended period of time. New voters appear at every election while some previous voters depart, not as reflections of shifting issue preferences or altered voter turnout, but as simple matters of life, death, and population replacement. On occasion, however, there is a reconstitution of the basic contours of the political community that is larger and more abrupt. This is most commonly a product of formal enfranchisement (or occasional disfranchisement), where the prime example is the most obvious step-change in overall influences on partisan alignment in all of postwar American politics.

This was the conscious (re)enfranchisement of black Americans in the 1960s, as part of a civil rights revolution.[1] Offshoots of this rights revolution would reach into most major aspects of American society, but its most directly political impact was on the formal definition of the American electorate. So any attempt to map out the changing evolution of partisan alignments in postwar American politics must turn to enfranchisement as a stimulus to partisan realignment, to civil rights as the policy domain impelling enfranchisement, and to racial background as the cleavage associated most centrally with both. This link between race and rights was hardly absent from prior American history. It was present at the constitutional founding; it was central to the Civil War and Reconstruction; it flared intermittently in the years that followed.[2] Yet few in the early postwar years foresaw the explosive manner in which it was about to reappear.

An Opening Alignment for Civil Rights

In the immediate postwar years, a survey asking about policy preferences on civil rights would have produced a set of obvious but weak parallels to the same story on social welfare (Table 2.1.A). Democrats collectively were on the left, but much more modestly than with welfare preferences. Republicans collectively were on the right, but likewise more modestly than for welfare preferences. The result was that the ideological distance between the two on civil rights was well

Table 2.1 Party Attachment, Racial Background, and Policy Preference: Civil Rights, 1950–1970

A. By Party		B. By Race	
Dems	−.08	Black	−.82
Reps	+.11	Nonblack	+.05

C. By Races within Parties	
Black Dems	−.82
Nonblack Dems	−.00
All Reps	+.11

short of the counterpart distance on social welfare—though whether this was a harbinger, where the politics of civil rights was a nascent version of the politics of social welfare, or just a transient relationship, small enough to move in a different direction at some later date, could not have been known from the direct linkage between policy preferences and party attachment.

Yet introducing the main social cleavage associated with policy preferences on civil rights, namely racial background, immediately renders that question more or less irrelevant, by clearly distinguishing the two domains[3] (Table 2.1.B). At the time, the notion of a racial minority centered on the distinction between black and nonblack Americans, and refocused this way, the division by racial background for policy preferences on civil rights dwarfs the counterpart division by party attachment. Black Americans were hugely cathected by issues of civil rights, while the nonblack majority as an aggregate had little interest in the matter, appearing ever so modestly conservative largely because the much smaller black minority was so uniformly and extremely liberal.

So the idea of a partisan alignment on civil rights as just a weaker version of the counterpart alignment on social welfare simply disappears. The next step in a conventional analysis of partisan alignments would be to look at the joint impact of party attachment and the relevant social cleavage, presumably yielding a fourfold table of policy preferences. Yet by the immediate postwar years, and well before the Civil Rights Act and the Voting Rights Act were to contribute a fresh racial increment to the American electorate, the population of black Republicans had dwindled to where it was too small for reliable measurement, even when sampled nationally. That left three racialized factions to produce the essential joint measures, and their story was clear.

Black Democrats contributed the ideological left, being overwhelmingly the reason that party attachment appeared initially to have organizing power on civil rights (Table 2.1.C). Yet nonblack Democrats, the largest of three factions, were pulled neither left nor right, sitting directly on the point of indifference, the national average. Republicans as a collectivity then provided a modest but clearly conservative ideological right, unaffected by their handful of black identifiers. And while nonblack Democrats were modestly left of these Republicans, this distance was tiny compared to the one between nonblack Democrats and their black fellow partisans.

That is an example of a policy alignment that was overwhelmingly demographic, with a whiff of partisanship at the margins, one very different from the counterpart alignment on social welfare. Or so these national figures would suggest. The addition of a regional focus in the following section will carve two of the three factional cohorts in additionally important ways. In the meantime, the prior question is whether black Americans, so unified and so dissident on civil rights, replicated this result in the other main policy domains. Would they show the same relationship to, for example, cultural values? Or conversely, would apparent differences by party on social welfare disappear if voters were further stratified by race?

To cut directly to the chase: the answer to both is no. Frequently the victims of racial discrimination with an economic impact, black Americans possessed a socially rooted policy interest that coincided with extreme liberalism on social welfare too, though these welfare preferences remained well short of black liberalism on civil rights[4] (Table 2.2.A). Yet this was hardly a generalized response, inherent to this social cleavage, and the best evidence came from the policy domain that would ultimately constitute the leading competitor for social welfare as an aligning principle for American politics, namely cultural values. Here, a racial analysis showed a black sample that was effectively indifferent, sitting almost directly on the national average.

So if the racial cleavage appeared determinative on civil rights, it was just as clearly relevant but not determinative on social welfare, while being nearly irrelevant on cultural values. Moreover, a return to looking at policy preferences the

Table 2.2 **Racial Background and Policy Domain: Social Welfare, Civil Rights, and Cultural Values, 1950–1970**

A. Among Black Americans

	1. Civil Rights	*2. Social Welfare*	*3. Cultural Values*
	−.82	−.53	−.02

B. By Races within Parties

	1. Civil Rights	*2. Social Welfare*	*3. Cultural Values*
Black Dems	−.82	−.53	−.01
Nonblack Dems	−.00	−.12	−.04
All Reps	+.11	+.11	+.04

Table 2.3 **Policy Preferences by Partisan Population: Civil Rights and Social Welfare, 1950–1970**

	DAcs	DRFs	RRFs	RAcs
Civil Rights	−.15	−.06	+.10	+.19
Social Welfare	−.19	−.17	+.20	+.39

other way around, that is, by racialized factions inside policy domains, features each of these domains aligning the three racialized factions in a different way (Table 2.2.B). On civil rights, demography was predominant, with just a hint of party among nonblacks. On social welfare, the same overall ordering appeared, but with a racial gap half that of civil rights and with the parties twice as far apart among nonblacks. And on cultural values, where a slight ideological difference did surface between nonblack Democrats and Republicans, this difference was larger than the one separating black Democrats from either of these other racial factions, while leaving them sitting on the national average.

The usual way to finish the introduction of a new policy domain and a fresh social cleavage is to ask about the four partisan populations as they embody—duplicate, alter, or deny—the diagnostic links between this policy realm, namely civil rights; this social cleavage, namely racial background; and party attachment. Table 2.3 does this in the interests of transparency and analytic comparison, though this is yet another case, like the relationship between party attachment and racial background, where the links between partisan populations and policy preferences will be recast in a major way in the next section by the intervening impact of geographic region.

Seen on their own, as partisan populations in the nation as a whole, the four populations again made civil rights look like a weak version of the counterpart story on social welfare. Both parties ran in the now-familiar direction, left to right from Democratic activists to the Democratic rank and file to the Republican rank and file to Republican activists. Activists were again more extreme than their putative constituencies, Democrats to the left and Republicans to the right. And these relationships were then tweaked in two noteworthy ways. In the first, every partisan population was more moderate on civil rights than on social welfare, suggesting that the former was more of a priority in American politics at the time.[5]

In the second tweak, Republican activists, who added individual distinction to the ideological continuum on social welfare by being the obvious and extreme outliers in policy preference, surrendered that distinction with civil rights. Instead, they were no farther right of their rank and file than were the Democratic activists at the other end of the ideological continuum. This is the first reminder of a party history where Republicans were originally the partisan champions of civil rights, a history that will return in the interpretation of regional alignments and then in the evolution of the national alignment over time.[6]

Regional Impacts on Partisan Alignments

Public preferences on social welfare in the immediate postwar years assumed an ideological alignment that was neatly organized both by party and by class for the nation as a whole. Ultimately, this result became a template for judging the nature and strength of partisan alignments in the other major domains. Yet even for social welfare, it was necessary to ask whether the national alignment was recapitulated in major geographic regions, and in one of the two, the American South, it was not. By party, the Southern Democrats were regionally distinctive. By class, the Southern upper class was regionally distinctive. Together, the two produced an ideological order for the four partisan populations that was itself distinctive, with Southern Democratic activists reliably out of alignment, and thus registered a further kind of regional exceptionalism.[7]

An initial look at public preferences on civil rights has already confirmed a different mix of aligning influences between the two domains, at least in this opening period. For civil rights, racial background proved to be a much stronger influence on a national alignment than social class had been for social welfare. Conversely, party attachment, the lead organizing influence on welfare alignments, was only a weak secondary influence in the rights domain. The latter was instead best characterized by a deep but narrow divide between black and nonblack Americans, deeper than the main social cleavage in any other policy domain though limited in its overall impact by the fact that one side of the cleavage encompassed only about 5% of the American electorate in these early postwar years.[8]

The simultaneous presence of geographic region as an aligning influence for social welfare would by itself have reinforced the need to ask about region in the rights domain. Even if it had not, the narrative of American politics at the time would surely have done so. In this narrative, civil rights and the racial cleavage were widely thought to contribute the defining divide between the political North and the political South,[9] which makes it unsurprising that where regional impacts had to be teased out and then carefully circumscribed on social welfare—which differences were and were not effectively regional?—region was to infuse every aspect of policy alignment on civil rights.

From the start, geographic region overwhelmed party attachment as an organizing principle (Table 2.4.A). The two more conservative populations were Southern Republicans and Southern Democrats, just as the two more liberal populations were Northern Democrats and Northern Republicans. And if Northern Democrats were the only ones truly left of the national average, the ideological distance from them to Southern Democrats was still double the size of the gap between Democrats and Republicans for the nation as a whole. So what

Civil Rights and Racial Background

Table 2.4 **Party Attachment, Racial Background, and Policy Preference: Civil Rights by Geographic Region, 1950–1970**

	A. By Party		B. By Race		
	Dems	Reps	Black	Nonblack	
North	−.19	+.08	−.87	−.02	North
South	+.16	+.32	−.60	+.32	South

C. By Races within Parties				
	Black Dems	Nonblack Dems	All Reps	
North	−.91	−.13	+.08	North
South	−.64	+.31	+.32	South

had been a conventional stratification by party attachment for social welfare, distinguished regionally by the comparative conservatism of Southern Democrats, was an archetypal divide by geographic region for civil rights, shaped clearly but only secondarily by party attachment.

Geographic region and racial background jousted in a different way, though there were some straightforward regularities: blacks more liberal than nonblacks in both regions, Southerners more conservative than Northerners in both races (Table 2.4.B). Yet a more politically useful summary would have to begin by noting that blacks were so far to the left of nonblacks as to trivialize the role of region among black Americans: they anchored the left on civil rights wherever they resided. Within the far larger nonblack majority, however, a regional gap in rights preferences remained substantial. Within this majority, Southern nonblacks were strongly conservative on civil rights, while Northern nonblacks fronted a position of indifference, tilted ever so slightly to the left. Southern nonblacks were still closer to Northern nonblacks than to either black population, North or South, however.

When the focus shifts to the three major racialized factions, it becomes clear that race dominated both region and party among blacks, while region distinguished nonblack Democrats and Republicans, and party had a further role to play only in the North (Table 2.5.C). Said the other way around, the gap between black and nonblack Democrats was huge in both regions. The gap between regions was present but inconsequential among black Democrats, evident and substantial among Republicans, and largest of all among nonblack Democrats. So the gap between parties was evident in the North, with Northern Democrats modestly liberal on civil rights and Northern Republicans modestly conservative. Yet this gap was nonexistent in the South, where both partisan groups were strongly—and indistinguishably—conservative.

Table 2.5 Partisan Populations and Policy Preferences: Civil Rights and Social Welfare by Region, 1950–1970

	DAcs	DRFs	RRFs	RAcs
A. North				
Civil Rights	−.26	−.18	+.07	+.14
Social Welfare	−.25	−.21	+.21	+.39
B. South				
Civil Rights	+.18	+.16	+.28	+.51
Social Welfare	+.02	−.06	+.14	+.49

What remains to complete this picture is to add the four partisan populations, yielding eight partisan cohorts when divided by region, where the result is about as striking a confirmation of the dominance of region over party as is possible to generate empirically (Table 2.5). With civil rights as with social welfare, region pulled each partisan population into more conservative territory in the South than in the North. With civil rights as with social welfare, Southern Democratic activists jumbled the resulting alignments further, by sitting to the left of their rank and file in the North but to its right in the South.

Yet those formal similarities look additionally and strikingly different when the scale of these Southern dissents re-enters the picture. And here, the ability to compare alignments for civil rights versus social welfare is particularly helpful. There is a distinctively Northern element to this rights story. In the North, the two Democratic populations stood in almost exactly the same position in both policy domains, while the two Republican populations differed clearly by domain. Northern Republicans were mildly conservative on civil rights and strongly conservative on social welfare, a Northern moderation on civil rights that will be important below, when the question becomes the evolution of these preferences over time.

But when the focus shifts not just to the fact but to the scale of Southern dissidence, this opening era sets an important benchmark for subsequent change, especially on civil rights and by comparison to the other policy domains. In the South, the two Democratic populations differed consistently as between civil rights and social welfare. In absolute terms, the Southern Democratic rank and file showed the largest difference between these two domains, being modestly liberal on social welfare and clearly conservative on civil rights. Southern Democratic activists also stood out for how far to the right they were willing to go on civil rights.

So for civil rights, region was an insistent presence when viewed through party attachment (Table 2.4.A). It was an insistent presence when viewed through racial background (Table 2.4.B). It was an insistent presence when viewed through the joint operation of the two (Table 2.4.C). And it remained an insistent presence among the four partisan populations, a fourth and final embodiment of the North/South divide (Table 2.5.A and B). As with social welfare, the North would again roughly copy the national pattern, in a modestly exaggerated fashion with the South removed from the analysis. But here and far more than with social welfare, the South would be the regional home of multiple and cascading deviations from national patterns.

The Evolution of a National Alignment

None of that—neither the full national setup in the immediate postwar years nor its regional pieces—can comment directly on the central engine of change in the rights domain, namely voter enfranchisement and an amended electorate. The passage of electoral reform occurred formally within the temporal bounds of the first postwar period, but its practical effects did not arrive seriously until the second. Hidden inside both the nation and its regional pieces during that first period were, by definition, some effects from the *absence* of the voters who would subsequently be enfranchised, along with the policy preferences that they would bring into electoral politics. But while there was plenty of argument in these prior years about what the impact of a changed electorate might be, there was by definition no evidence of this prospective impact.

There is no evidence, that is, until it actually arrived in its single largest incarnation during all the years after World War II. This was courtesy of the Voting Rights Act of 1965, as a follow-on to the Civil Rights Act of 1964.[10] The theoretically targeted group was black Americans, and fresh black enfranchisees were to be the largest practical addition to a consciously altered electorate, though there must have been additional voting increments from previously enfranchised blacks who were stimulated to exercise their franchise by the battle over civil rights, from nonblacks who had previously been collateral damage from voting restrictions aimed most pointedly at black Americans, and from nonblacks whose attention was likewise captured by a civil rights revolution, not necessarily in a supportive fashion.

Even by the crudest of measures, namely black versus nonblack shares of the total electorate, the social shift in the aftermath of reform was substantial. The black share of this electorate actually doubled between the first postwar era and the second (Table 2.6.A). To find a larger numerical impact from formal enfranchisement, the analyst would probably have to go back to women's suffrage and the Nineteenth Amendment, ratified in 1920.[11] Moreover, the black share that was jumpstarted by a legal revolution in civil rights during the 1960s would continue to rise, albeit less dramatically, adding a further 40% to its proportion of the total electorate in the succeeding era.

Yet when the focus is not the racial composition of the electorate but the racial composition of the major parties, this effect was profoundly bifurcated (Table 2.6.B). Among Democrats, the party of choice among existing black voters, the black share of party identifiers likewise doubled between the first and the second postwar eras, coming close to one in five Democratic partisans. That share would continue to rise in the successor period, up a further third and coming to constitute one in four Democrats overall.[12] Among Republicans, however, the black share of party identifiers actually declined, vacillating between 2%-minus and 1%-plus for the entire postwar period. On one side, then, a massive influx of new voters remade the Democratic Party. On the other side, there was not even a social echo within their Republican opposition.

Striking as that partisan divergence is, however, it still partially masks the compositional implications of an augmented black electorate. In the old and unreformed world, it was already clear that the parties needed to be treated not as two grand blocs but rather as three great factions when race was the focus: black Democrats, nonblack Democrats, and (all) Republicans. If not, aggregation by party, especially in the case of the Democrats, would meld two socially disparate stories, nowhere more critically than in the realm of civil rights. So looked at this way, across factions rather than just within parties, there almost had to be three and not just two demographic impacts from voter enfranchisement.

The first, most deliberate, and most obvious still belonged to black Americans (Table 2.6.B). Their numbers doubled, their Democratic share doubled, yet their Republican share was static. Had there been no change among nonblack

Table 2.6 **Racial Demographics: Percent Black across Time**

	A. In the Electorate	B. In the Parties		
	as a Whole	Dems	Reps	
E3	14%	24%	2%	E3
E2	10%	18%	1%	E2
E1	5%	9%	2%	E1

C. By Races within Parties

	Black Dems	Nonblack Dems	All Reps	
E3	14%	44%	42%	E3
E2	10%	45%	46%	E2
E1	5%	54%	41%	E1

Americans in this second era, the other two factions, namely nonblack Democrats plus Republicans, would have declined in some mix that added up to this 5% gain by their black fellow citizens. But in fact, the share of the Republicans also increased substantially, from 41% to 46%. So while a 5% gain loomed proportionately larger among black Americans, the same gain applied to a larger absolute population of Republicans was sufficient to elevate the party as a whole from minority to plurality status among the three racialized factions.

Inevitably, if both Republicans and black Democrats were gaining electoral shares, nonblack Democrats had to be paying a proportionate price. Beginning with 54% of the total in the first era—a national majority all by itself—this third faction fell to 45% in the second era. This proved, however, to be a dramatic but conditional result, since the factional balance would be tickled once again in the third postwar period. Black Democrats would continue to gain. But this time, it was Republicans who shed some of their gains from the preceding era, with the result that nonblack Democrats achieved an ironic result, restoring their position as the modal faction for the country as a whole while continuing to decline as a share of the total electorate.

With that as demographic background, the policy domain most directly driving and being driven by a conscious effort to alter the composition of the electorate remained civil rights, where the central question is what was happening to the initial partisan alignment during this huge enfranchisement and associated transition to a different racial balance.[13] And the first thing to say is that the two parties in the aggregate were polarizing about equally on civil rights, with Democrats farther left and Republicans farther right (Table 2.7.A). The scope of this overall partisan polarization, that is, the distance between aggregate Democrats and aggregate Republicans, nearly doubled in the second postwar period, apart from any consideration of the contribution of racialized factions inside the two parties.

Disentangled by race, however, there was a good deal more to say (Table 2.7.B). In the first postwar era, black Democrats had contributed the far ideological left, Republicans had contributed a modest ideological right, and nonblack

Table 2.7 **Party Attachment, Racial Background, and Policy Preference: Civil Rights across the Postwar Period**

	A. By Party		B. By Racialized Factions		
	Dems	Reps	Black Dems	Nonblack Dems	All Reps
Era 3	−.24	+.36	−.69	−.12	+.36
Era 2	−.16	+.19	−.91	+.00	+.19
Era 1	−.08	+.12	−.83	−.00	+.12

Democrats stood in the true center. Remarkably, much the same could still be said after the greatest electoral transformation of the entire postwar period. Black Democrats still contributed a distant left, even more so as new electoral additions proved not to be a moderating influence. Republicans now constituted a less modest right, shifting opposite to black Democrats. And the nonblack Democrats continued to sit directly on the national average, still manifesting aggregate indifference to civil rights as a policy domain. This means that the aggregate move leftward by the Democratic Party as a whole was overwhelmingly a product of the growing cohort of black Democrats.

In the subsequent shift into the modern world, all this would be sweepingly recast. The two parties would continue to polarize, even more vigorously (Table 2.7.A), though this time, a full two-thirds of the increase was to be contributed by Republicans rather than Democrats. Among racialized factions, black Democrats would continue to stake out the ideological left, less extremely than in the preceding period but still in an ideological world all their own (Table 2.7.B). Yet the big news came from the nonblack Democrats, abandoning the center and becoming cautiously liberal. In the process, they contributed all of the leftward move by the Democratic Party as a whole. At the same time and lastly, the Republicans abandoned a historical moderation on civil rights and became the clear conservatives, if still closer to the national average than black Democrats.

By extension, the critical faction—the fulcrum for change—differed from era to era. For the first postwar change, from the first to the second eras, it was black Democrats, whose arrival as a numerically serious faction drove ideological realignment. They remained extremely liberal on civil rights; that did not change. It was just that there were now twice as many of them. In the subsequent shift into the modern world, however, this pivotal role was split between Republicans and nonblack Democrats. Republicans claimed the largest aggregate shift. Having remained in the shadow of an ancestral moderation on civil rights in the second period, they finally gave it up in the third. Yet nonblack Democrats made arguably the more striking change, moving all the way across the national average from conservative to liberal.

But how much of these noteworthy changes was ideological, due to changing policy preferences among established voters, and how much was demographic, owed to a changing social composition of the electorate itself? As ever, it is impossible to answer definitively without being able to follow the same individuals across time. Still, it is easy to produce a benchmark estimate by accepting that the three racialized factions in any given era held the policy preferences that sample surveys showed them to hold but applying these preferences to the social composition of the preceding rather than the current period. In this way, it becomes possible to parse ideological change into a component that follows

Table 2.8 **The Impact of Enfranchisement: Civil Rights across the Postwar Period**

	Era 1	Era 2	Era 2 as E1	Era 3	Era 3 as E2
Dems	−.08	−.16	−.10	−.24	−.24
Reps	+.12	+.19	+.20	+.36	+.36

mechanically from an altered electorate versus a component that gathers the revised preferences of an unchanged social base.

From the start, these recalculations had nearly nothing to say about the evolution of the Republican Party. Because it began with a tiny black constituency, one that did not grow in either of the two succeeding eras, a recalculation based on race per se could have little effect (Table 2.8). There must have been some very real change inside the party on civil rights that resulted from in-migration among nonblack Democrats whose policy preferences accorded more with Republican positions, just as there must have been some change that resulted from out-migration by Republicans who found Democratic policy preferences more congenial. But a recalculation by race is irrelevant to both. Unsurprisingly, then, Republican recalculations for the second postwar era (+.19 versus +.20) or the modern world (+.36 versus +.36) were clearly not directly altered by changing racial composition in either era.

Yet on the other side of the partisan aisle, a growing body of black identifiers and a shifting balance between blacks and nonblacks allow these recalculations to tell a very different story. On civil rights, the Democratic Party as a whole doubled its distance from the national average between the first and the second postwar eras, where a full three-quarters of this change can be assigned to altered racial composition (Table 2.8.A). An unchanged social base would still have moved modestly leftward, from −.08 to −.10. But all the rest, from −.10 to −.16, can be accounted for by an altered racial balance. Yet that was also to be the end of this compositional story. In the shift from the second postwar era to the third, racial composition by itself had nothing further to contribute. The party did make another major move leftward, from −.16 to −.24, equal in scope to the move between the first and second periods. But all of this further shift had to be assigned to changing preferences; none could be chalked up to an altered racial composition.

The final step in examining the evolution of a national alignment on civil rights involves breaking the two parties into four partisan populations and tracking the intraparty politics that appears. In the opening postwar period, a national alignment by partisan population on civil rights did run in a fashion parallel to the one on social welfare, from Democratic activists to the Democratic rank and file

THE SOCIAL ROOTS OF AMERICAN POLITICS

Table 2.9 **Policy Preferences by Partisan Population: Civil Rights across the Postwar Period**

A. All Partisans

	DAcs	DRFs	RRFs	RAcs
Era 3	−.42	−.22	+.34	+.45
Era 2	−.39	−.12	+.18	+.22
Era 1	−.15	−.06	+.10	+.19

B. Nonblacks Only

	DAcs	DRFs	RRFs	RAcs
Era 3	−.33	−.07	+.36	+.45
Era 2	−.30	+.07	+.20	+.22
Era 1	−.08	+.01	+.11	+.20

to the Republican rank and file to Republican activists (Table 2.9.A). Unlike social welfare, however, where Republican activists were sharply off to the right, the two sets of party activists were roughly symmetric in their rights preferences. Stratified by race, what was additionally noteworthy was the racial divide among rank-and-file Democrats (Table 2.9.B). Their modest liberalism on civil rights proved to be more or less entirely due to the small cohort of black Democrats within their ranks.

For the nation as a whole, the two rank-and-file populations were to polarize impressively during the second postwar period, moving about the same distance for both, while doubling the ideological distance between them as they did so (Table 2.9.A). The two activist populations were doing something very different. Republican activists moved only modestly to the right, and since the Republican rank and file was moving clearly rightward at the same time, the two Republican populations were effectively converging. Yet Democratic activists were diving off to the left on civil rights, tripling the gap between themselves and their rank and file and becoming as extreme on civil rights in this second period as Republican activists had been on social welfare in the first.

But this time, a further look under the racial blanket is essential to interpreting these figures. Once again, it was the nonblack Democratic rank and file, not the Republicans and not black Democrats, that was central to a big racial difference in the second period (Table 2.9.B). In the aggregate, the Democratic rank and file was to double its collective liberalism between the first and the second eras. Yet at the same time, the nonblack rank and file moved clearly *to the right*, making this the population with by far the greatest ideological difference between the sample as a whole and a nonblack sample within it. Said the other way around, the increasing liberalism of the rank-and-file Democratic Party was purely the product of racial enfranchisement, actively resisted by the nonblack rank and file.

Only in the third postwar era did this Democratic rank and file come into orthodox alignment with the three other partisan populations. The two rank and files continued to polarize (Table 2.9.A), as did the two active parties, though the Republican move to the right was much larger than the Democratic move to the left this time. On the one hand, the Democratic rank and file was now clearly liberal, and far from the Republican rank and file. On the other hand, it was still the most moderate of the four partisan populations, as well as the one where it was most important to distinguish black from nonblack identifiers (Table 2.9.B).

Regional Contributions to an Evolving National Picture

Geographic region had been not just a consequential influence on partisan alignments involving civil rights in the immediate postwar years. It was the main organizing principle for these alignments. Far beyond just outweighing party attachment, region went on to organize all four partisan populations by a different leading principle, not Democrat versus Republican but South versus North. Yet the social cleavage most closely associated with policy preferences on civil rights, namely racial background, also trumped party attachment as an organizing influence in that opening period, carving the parties into racialized factions: black Democrats, nonblack Democrats, and Republicans. And here, the numerical balance among these factions was destined to be critical to any overall policy alignment on civil rights.[14]

Those three background influences, namely party attachment, geographic region, and racialized faction, were all in play inside the voter enfranchisement that would distinguish the second postwar period. From the other side, a changing partisan alignment on civil rights would be the crucial measure of the power of enfranchisement as a change engine. The Civil Rights Act of 1964 opened the door to this possibility, but it was the Voting Rights Act of 1965 that brought it to fruition: an altered racial composition to the voting electorate being its central aim. Yet the black population of the United States was geographically concentrated in the South, and while there would be migration currents and crosscurrents among blacks and nonblacks across all the years to come, the black population would still be concentrated in the South in the modern era. So region, race, and party were inescapably entwined in the impact of voting reform.

Three separable impacts are needed to tell this story. By race, the black share of the electorate increased impressively in the aftermath of reform, more than

54 THE SOCIAL ROOTS OF AMERICAN POLITICS

doubling as a share of the voting populace for the nation as a whole. Yet by region, the implications of this increase differed substantially. A doubling in the North would take the black electoral share from 4% to 9%, but a doubling in the South would take it from 11% to 24%[15] (Table 2.10.A). By party, finally, this shifting racial balance would be further bifurcated. New black voters flocked to the Democrats and bypassed the Republicans, so the Democratic Party was remade through voter enfranchisement, while impacts on the Republican Party were only indirect and gradual (Table 2.10.B).

Racialized party factions then summarize this collective story[16] (Table 2.10.C). For the nation as a whole, nonblack Democrats had possessed an actual majority in the first postwar period. Republicans would then surge to a plurality in the second period. And nonblack Democrats would displace them as a plurality, though never again as a majority, in the modern era. Inevitably, region was integral to these effects too. By definition, a Democratic Party that would end up 20% black in the North but 40% black in the South would present a different factional array by region. Yet the final result would be ironic: the specifics of black enfranchisement, as they ramified through the two other racialized factions, would be central to a *nationalization* of partisan alignments.

The North roughly copied the national story, while being a bit more Republican and considerably less black throughout. In this, the North offered a majority to nonblack Democrats in the opening period, a majority to Republicans in the successor era, and a plurality to nonblack Democrats in the

Table 2.10 **Racial Demographics by Region: Percent Black across Time**

	A. In the Electorate		B. In the Parties				
	1. North	*2. South*	*1. North*		*2. South*		
			Dems	Reps	Dems	Reps	
Era 3	9%	24%	19%	1%	38%	3%	Era 3
Era 2	6%	19%	12%	1%	28%	4%	Era 2
Era 1	4%	11%	7%	1%	13%	5%	Era 1

C. Racial Background by Party Faction

	1. North			2. South			
	Black Dems	Nonblack Dems	All Reps	Black Dems	Nonblack Dems	All Reps	
Era 3	9%	47%	44%	22%	37%	41%	Era 3
Era 2	6%	44%	50%	18%	46%	36%	Era 2
Era 1	4%	50%	46%	10%	65%	25%	Era 1

modern world.[17] But the South was the site of the action when voter enfranchisement is the focus. A counterpart Southern story began with a crushing preponderance of nonblack Democrats. They remained the plurality in the successor period, though Southern Republicans began to show serious signs of life, while black Democrats increased in an even greater proportion. Lastly, for the modern South, it would be the Republicans who secured a regional plurality, with black Democrats continuing to rise and nonblack Democrats continuing to decline.[18]

Viewed through the lens of regional parties—Northern Democrats, Northern Republicans, Southern Democrats, and Southern Republicans—both the Northern Democrats and the Southern Republicans would see little change (Table 2.11.A.1 and 2). Northern Democrats would begin and remain clearly liberal; Southern Republicans would begin and remain strongly conservative; neither would move much over time. Once more, the Southern Democrats would be the heart of the story, though this time, Northern Republicans would be consequential as well. Beginning as clearly conservative and aggressively dissident, the Southern Democrats would come into conformity with the national alignment in the middle period, while ending up as literally the most liberal regional party. Yet Northern Republicans would feature a major odyssey in the opposite direction, moving from modestly to strongly conservative while doubling their distance from the national average in each succeeding period.

Table 2.11 **Geographic Region and Policy Preference: Civil Rights across the Postwar Period**

A. By Party

	1. North		2. South		
	Dems	Reps	Dems	Reps	
Era 3	−.23	+.33	−.32	+.37	Era 3
Era 2	−.22	+.17	−.11	+.29	Era 2
Era 1	−.19	+.08	+.18	+.33	Era 1

B. By Races within Parties

	1. North			2. South			
	Black Dems	Nonblack Dems	All Reps	Black Dems	Nonblack Dems	All Reps	
Era 3	−.74	−.13	+.33	−.66	−.12	+.37	Era 3
Era 2	−.60	−.10	+.17	−.90	+.20	+.29	Era 2
Era 1	−.88	−.13	+.08	−.60	+.31	+.35	Era 1

In stages, then, the overall result would be a civil rights alignment that achieved a generalized regional conformity in the second postwar era, going on to be as sharply polarized by party as any policy domain in the third. What was going on inside these partisan realignments, converging across regions while diverging by party? To answer that question, the three racial factions must return to play an important role in driving change—and unpacking its details. The Republican story, being largely unaffected by internal racial divisions, was to be a combination of two sharply different regional trajectories (Table 2.11.A.1 and 2). Southern Republicans began and remained conservative on civil rights; they were a case of ideological stasis buttressed by surging numerical growth.[19] By contrast, Northern Republicans began as the most moderate regional faction, inheritors of a time-honored if ebbing support for civil rights. Yet era by era, they would close the gap with their Southern counterparts. So those were two simple but opposite stories of regional convergence.

Still, the larger factional story began and remained inside the Democratic Party. In the North, nonblack Democrats started out as moderately liberal, where they essentially stayed for the next half-century[20] (Table 2.11.B.1). Black Democrats began as very liberal and stayed there as well, never coming close to their nonblack co-partisans. By contrast, the South would feature a convulsive change, with trajectories specific to the racialized factions (Table 2.11.B.2). Black Southern Democrats did wander a bit from era to era, moving leftward during the great enfranchisement, retrenching a bit in the modern era. Yet this was to be coupled with the largest move on the part of any faction—a fundamental change in ideological positioning—on the part of nonblack Southern Democrats.

Their historic shift into national conformity was actually lagged, arriving in two temporal pieces. In the second postwar era, there was little to see from nonblack Democratic identifiers. It was an expanded black electorate that provided the push for regional realignment in this period, which made the third era, the modern period, stand out. Only then did nonblack Democrats join the national alignment, though when they did, their newfound liberalism was sufficient to fuel a clearly augmented partisan polarization.[21] Moving sharply left of their previous position, these nonblack Southern Democrats became indistinguishable from nonblack Northern Democrats in their policy preferences on civil rights.

What gave these nonblack Southern Democrats such an impressively lagged but ultimately decisive role in driving Southern conformity with a national alignment on civil rights? Even more than with a national sample, the focus on one racial group within one party in one region is beyond the capacity of an ANES survey to distinguish individual moves. Yet it is possible to ask where these individuals stood collectively with respect to national party positions on major policy issues. To that end, Table 2.12 recovers the share of nonblack

Civil Rights and Racial Background 57

Table 2.12 **Misaligned Populations: Nonblack Southern Democrats**

	Civil Rights	*Social Welfare*	
Era 3	26%	14%	Era 3
Era 2	49%	27%	Era 2
Era 1	56%	30%	Era 1

Southern Democrats who were misaligned by party attachment in each postwar era. These are the Democratic identifiers whose policy preferences were to the right of rank-and-file Republicans on civil rights or social welfare. The resulting story suggests that many were coming into line with national party positions on civil rights and that some of those who did not were nevertheless held in the Democratic Party by their preferences on social welfare, where they were always better (more accurately) aligned.

Nonblack Southern Democrats were better aligned by party with regard to social welfare as opposed to civil rights in every postwar period. This difference looked additionally striking in the second period, when nearly half of the nonblack Southern Democrats could reasonably have been Republican by rights preference. Yet by the third period, in the modern era, both policy misalignments had fallen sharply. At the least, a change this large left room for some to shift their policy preferences toward their chosen party, while others changed their party attachment. Moreover, the counterpart figures for social welfare, showing nonblack Southern Democrats in good alignment with their national party by the modern era, imply that welfare preferences may have kept racial dissidents in their previously chosen party in spite of any remaining misalignment on civil rights.

Voter Enfranchisement as a Change Engine

So an evolutionary picture of rights alignments was influenced from one side by demographic change, through new voters produced by voter (re)enfranchisement, while from the other side, the same picture was influenced by programmatic change, from shifting policy preferences among established voters. To provide a more explicit measure of their comparative influence, we can return to a familiar analytic technique. As before, this involves accepting the expressed preferences of three racialized factions, now stratified by region, but applying these preferences to the racial distributions that had characterized these parties and their regions in the previous as well as the contemporary periods.

58 THE SOCIAL ROOTS OF AMERICAN POLITICS

Given the bifurcated character of party loyalties among newly enfranchised voters, there was little room for direct additions to Republican preferences from voting reform itself, and none surfaced (Table 2.13.A and B). There was in fact nearly no difference between Republican preferences calculated on the old versus the new racial distributions. This was true in the second postwar period; it was true in the third period; it was true in the North; and it was true in the South. Southern Republicans remained considerably more conservative than Northern Republicans on civil rights during the second period, but by the modern era, even that difference was residual. The two regional Republican Parties had essentially converged.

Among Democrats, there was more to see, albeit disproportionately in the South (Table 2.13.A and B). In the North, impacts from alternative calculations were in the expected direction but marginal. In the second era, a revised social base would have been sufficient to move the party from −.21 to −.22; in the third era, the same driver would have moved the party onward from −.22 to −.23. This meant that there was only minimal contribution to partisan alignments from racial enfranchisement among Northern Republicans, Southern Republicans, and even Northern Democrats. Yet the Southern Democrats would more than make up for this lack of reform impact, both by comparison to their own policy preferences across time and through their contribution to bringing the region as a whole into national alignment.

This was especially true in the second era, the one driven most directly by electoral reform. At that point, the Southern Democratic Party moved all the way from clearly conservative in the first postwar era to clearly liberal in the second on civil rights. Yet here, the larger half of a critical shift was due to a changing social composition rather than changing policy preferences. Without electoral reform, that is, with policy preferences on civil rights as they were in

Table 2.13 **The Impact of Enfranchisement: Eras, Regions, and Partisan Preferences on Civil Rights**

A. North

	Era 1	Era 2	Era 2 as E1	Era 3	Era 3 as E2
Dems	−.19	−.22	−.21	−.23	−.20
Reps	+.08	+.17	+.16	+.33	+.34

B. South

	Era 1	Era 2	Era 2 as E1	Era 3	Era 3 as E2
Dems	+.18	−.11	+.05	−.32	−.27
Reps	+.33	+.29	+.29	+.37	+.38

Civil Rights and Racial Background 59

the second era but calculated on the social composition of the first, the Southern Democratic Party would still have moved leftward, from +.18 to +.05. But the larger half of its move, from +.05 to −.11, would not have occurred. So a new rights liberalism was more the product of voter enfranchisement. Moreover, despite this dramatic impact from electoral reform, its ongoing effect was not finished. The South was to move farther leftward in the third period, and while the larger half of this move was a product of liberalizing policy preferences (−.11 to −.27), there remained a serious secondary contribution from demographic change (−.27 to −.32).

That leaves only the question of the impact of these changes on internal party politics, that is, on the four partisan populations inside the two regional party systems (Table 2.14.A). What had made the South so extreme and so dissident at the start was that the alignment produced by these Southern populations did not even overlap with the one from the North. Not only was each Southern population right of each Northern counterpart, but also the entire Southern alignment was right of the entire Northern alignment. That dissident regional picture changed in the succeeding era, superficially dismissing an old Southern dissent. Yet showing this particular change from both sides of the racial divide will make it clear that regional realignment remained partial and thus potentially unstable in this second postwar period.

Without further attention to this racial divide, the two regional alignments, North and South, appeared to overlap fully and in the orthodox fashion. Each

Table 2.14 **Policy Preference by Partisan Population: Civil Rights across the Postwar Period by Region**

A. All Partisans

	1. North				2. South			
	DAcs	*DRFs*	*RRFs*	*RAcs*	*DAcs*	*DRFs*	*RRFs*	*RAcs*
Era 3	−.46	−.18	+.34	+.42	−.35	−.28	+.34	+.50
Era 2	−.42	−.16	+.16	+.20	−.33	−.07	+.29	+.30
Era 1	−.25	−.18	+.06	+.15	+.18	+.18	+.28	+.51

B. Nonblacks Only

	1. North				2. South			
	DAcs	*DRFs*	*RRFs*	*RAcs*	*DAcs*	*DRFs*	*RRFs*	*RAcs*
Era 3	−.34	−.09	+.34	+.42	−.29	−.04	+.38	+.51
Era 2	−.37	−.02	+17	+.20	−.06	+.24	+.32	+.31
Era 1	−.22	−.12	+.07	+.16	+.28	+.31	+.34	+.54

Democratic population was left of its Republican counterpart, and all Democratic populations were left of all Republican populations, apparently eliminating the old regional chasm between policy alignments inside the two parties (Table 2.14.A). Yet a further isolation of nonblacks suggests just how limited this new surface conformity was. With black Democrats removed from the sample, only (nonblack) Democratic activists were actually liberal—left of center—and this put them in tension with what was otherwise still a purely regional alignment (Table 2.14.B). Seen this way, the other *three* partisan populations in the South were still right of every Northern population, including both Northern Republican pieces.

Most critically, the nonblack Southern Democratic rank and file, the core of the regional party, remained in dissent, being not just conservative on its own terms but still right of its Northern *Republican* counterpart. So the reality of a full change among aggregate parties, the change that superficially characterized the second postwar period, had to wait until the modern era. Only then did change in the nonblack Southern Democracy finally cement the South into an ongoing national alignment. Said differently, the superficial shift that surfaced in the second era became political reality only in the third. For the two parties as collective wholes, black and nonblack, Republican and Democratic, there was now a neatly ordered and strongly polarized alignment encompassing both major regions and all four partisan populations (Table 2.14.A).

In fact, the population closest to being ideologically out of place was now the Northern Democratic rank and file, coming in as less liberal than its Southern counterpart. Stripped of their black partisans, that is, among nonblacks only, the dissent of the Southern Democratic rank and file, a dissent that had made an emerging commonality by geographic region still highly contingent in the second postwar period, had disappeared. This nonblack Southern Democratic rank and file remained the most moderate partisan population in the nation, sitting just left of the national average. But even this was in the orthodox ideological position, left of center and left of all four Republican populations. Along the way, the last vestiges of a partisan alignment that had once been the great distinction to Southern regional politics had finally disappeared.

Enfranchisement, Electorates, Race, and Rights

At the end of the Second World War, social welfare was widely recognized as the programmatic centerpiece of American politics, and the associated partisan alignment was to provide a template for judging and comparing the structure of this politics for all the major policy domains across all the postwar years.

Inside this template was a lasting triumvirate, linking a dominant *social cleavage* in the form of social class to *public preferences* on welfare policy gathered by *party attachment*, with Democrats to the left and Republicans to the right. This linkage would grow only stronger as time passed, yet if any of the analysts who recognized the early partisan alignment on social welfare assumed that it would naturally be copied in other policy domains, they should have been immediately disabused by observing the counterpart alignment for civil rights.

By definition, the rights domain featured a different policy focus. In practice, rights preferences sprang from a different social cleavage as well. Yet that cleavage, racial background, was to dominate party attachment as an organizing principle in the early postwar years, snuffing out superficial parallels to social welfare. Indeed, and very unlike social class, race did not have to realize its aligning potential through the political parties. Rather, parties had to realize whatever organizing potential they could salvage by means of racial factions. Black Democrats and black Republicans, where the latter could be found, were nearly indistinguishable in their (very liberal) rights preferences. Nonblack Democrats and nonblack Republicans were likewise little different, the modest apparent liberalism of the Democratic Party being largely residual, stemming from the fact that most blacks were Democrats.

So it was racialized factions that gave this second major domain an initial alignment. Yet there was another major principle for organizing public preferences on civil rights, one that drove everything except minority racial status into a distant second place. This alternative principle was geographic region, in the form of the historic North/South divide, and it was to infuse every remaining aspect of policy alignment in the rights domain. Black Democrats in the North and South actually differed little by region, while the paucity of black Republicans made a partisan comparison among black Americans of little consequence. But among the nonblack majority, civil rights in these early years provided the greatest single embodiment in the entire survey era of the ability of geographic region to shape policy preferences in a distinctive fashion.

Region overwhelmed party attachment in aligning these nonblack Americans. With civil rights as with social welfare, the South pulled every aspect of a North/South comparison in the conservative direction. Yet for civil rights, this difference was extreme. By party attachment, the two more liberal parties were Northern Democrats and Northern Republicans; the two more conservative parties—and far more conservative at that—were Southern Republicans and Southern Democrats. By extension, region went on to overwhelm any further shaping influence from party structure. Among the partisan populations, all four Northern cohorts were left of all four Southern counterparts, such that even Republican activists in the North were left of Democratic activists from the South. That was region over party with a vengeance.

62 THE SOCIAL ROOTS OF AMERICAN POLITICS

Yet if civil rights was distinguished by the initial organizing power of region, it was also to produce the most far-reaching *change* in shaping influences on partisan alignment, courtesy of the greatest conscious reform in the boundaries of the political community for the entire postwar period. The legislative underpinnings of this formal change lay in the Voting Rights Act of 1965. The major beneficiaries were its target constituency, black Americans. And the rapid increase in their numerical presence in the electorate, along with a chain of responses to that increase by other groups, would lead to the far-reaching realignment of civil rights. Seen the other way around, civil rights was to demonstrate the power of voter enfranchisement as a change engine, directly through the changed demographic composition of the political community but also indirectly through subsequent strategic adjustments among all the major pieces of that community.

The directly numerical effect of reform was huge. The black share of voters for the nation as a whole doubled in the second postwar period, then increased a further 40% in the third. The partisan impact of this change was, however, immediately bifurcated, with the Democratic Party more than matching these overall changes in racial balance, while the Republican Party showed little trace of direct demographic impact. Key further changes inside this bifurcated shift had to be captured through racialized factions: black Democrats, nonblack Democrats, and Republicans:

- In the old world, nonblack Democrats had been a simple majority of American voters, needing no one else to ensure their majority.
- In the successor period, black Democrats jumped up strongly but so did Republicans, who actually became the plurality faction.
- In the modern era, nonblack Democrats continued to decline but returned to plurality leadership on their way down.
- There remained a regional tweak to these demographic developments, however:
  1. The North roughly followed the national story, with fewer new black voters and somewhat more Republicans.
  2. The South gained the lion's share of new black voters but suffered the larger decline among nonblack Democrats.

All that said, the central analytic question remains the impact of changing demographic composition and shifting factional preferences on partisan alignments. This impact was to arrive in what proved to be a two-step process. Change began with an explosion of new black voters in the second postwar period, confirming the power of voter enfranchisement as a change engine, though this would not be the end of that influence: a second demographic wave would follow in the third era. In the second period, however, the lead story was directly demographic, involving the strong policy preferences on civil rights brought into American politics by a burgeoning electoral base of black Democrats.

Yet this second postwar period also saw the Republican Party ease away from its historical moderation in the rights domain while at long last securing serious growth in the South. With hindsight, this would remind both analysts and participants that a substantial change in any major piece of the political community was likely to generate—in truth, it likely required—substantial adjustments by all the rest. So while there must have been some new voters who arrived as Republicans, Republican change basically involved a response to the huge new (black) Democratic increment. And all the while, nonblack Democrats essentially marked time, staying with their aggregate ideological indifference.

The resulting change in this second postwar period was nevertheless impressive in statistical terms; it would be hard to find another postwar reform that approximated its practical impact. Yet this direct result impelled only a limited restructuring of overall partisan alignments, limited in two senses. In the first, direct demographic change was occurring intensely but narrowly, that is, within one racial faction. In a second limitation, a look under the racial blanket showed that those apparently neutral rank-and-file Democrats were split deeply along racial lines. Black Democrats were pulling the rank and file strenuously to the left. But nonblack Democrats were simultaneously moving to the right, ending up closer not just to the Republican rank and file but to Republican activists rather than to their own (putative) activists on civil rights.

That was the first step in an overarching process of change. The second step was to be different, so different as to bring a comprehensive realignment to the rights domain while pulling this new alignment into full conformity with the existing alignment on social welfare. Black Democrats again increased their numbers while retaining strongly liberal preferences. But this time, Republicans moved much more actively to the right, creating an obvious home for conservatives, or for those who just gave civil rights a lower priority than social welfare, cultural values, or national security. And crucially, nonblack Democrats, long the policy pivot in this domain, abandoned their previously reflexive centrism and were reborn as moderately liberal.

How had this happened? Available data cannot answer the question of who specifically—which individuals—moved in order to bring a modern partisan alignment to the rights domain. But it is not hard to isolate the social group that made the crucial collective move. Demographic change alone made nonblack Democrats the critical pivot. Black Democrats were growing, Republicans were growing, and if nonblack Democrats were correspondingly in decline, they were more than ever the swing population. Moreover, we can know that among these nonblack Democrats, there was a huge subset of misaligned partisans, that is,

Democratic identifiers whose policy preferences on civil rights were closer to—actually to the right of—rank-and-file Republicans.

So it was the misaligned, nonblack, rank-and-file Democrats who had to change, *if* a new and comprehensive partisan alignment was to be produced in the modern era. Said the other way around, these misalignments were what had to be "ironed out" if there was to be a transition to a comprehensive partisan alignment for civil rights that ran parallel to the one on social welfare. Misaligned Democrats had declined only minimally in the second period, when voter enfranchisement was the story and demographic shifts were the driving force. But in the modern era, where shifting policy preferences were the story instead, the number of misaligned Democrats was cut literally in half. As with social welfare in the second period, so with civil rights in the modern era: the position of the national parties had become indisputable.

So if change had to come principally among misaligned nonblack rank-and-file Democrats, it had to arrive either by coming into line with the dominant values of the Democratic Party or by switching allegiance to the Republicans—or, of course, both. Every expression of this change was to be greater in the South than in the North: greater black enfranchisement, greater division by race within the Democratic rank and file, greater change by this rank and file in the modern world. Yet in the end, the regions too had converged in their partisan alignments on civil rights, while the overall rights alignment converged with a now-parallel alignment on social welfare.

Inside that overall story, Northern Democrats and Southern Republicans had been only marginally affected. They would stand at the end roughly where they had stood in the beginning. Northern Republicans had moved clearly to the right, doubling their ideological distance from the national average in the second era, then doubling it again in the third. Southern Democrats, however, still made the greatest move of all, changing from clearly conservative in the opening period, to modestly liberal in the second period, to marginally the most liberal among rank-and-file partisan cohorts in the modern world.

As Republicans moved right and nonblack Democrats moved left, party attachment became increasingly consequential, now for civil rights and not just social welfare. As party attachment rose as an organizing principle for rights preferences and not just welfare preferences, geographic region inevitably declined, retaining a bit more influence on policy preferences for civil rights than for social welfare. And the power of racial background retained a greater autonomous influence on *one side* of the racial cleavage than any individual class did with social welfare, though the class divide was omnipresent, much larger, and always consequential. Yet in the end, it was the convergence between partisan alignments across the two domains that remained most impressive.

3

Partisan Mobilization and Policy Alignment

Cultural Values and Religious Denominations

Social welfare was the policy focus and social class the dominant cleavage in the lone partisan alignment that was already in place in American politics when the postwar era began, one destined to be diagnostic and long-lasting. Civil rights became the policy focus and racial background the dominant cleavage for the first major addition to this enduring picture, likewise lasting though only incipient when the postwar period arrived. Three conclusions follow. One is that as dominant as social welfare was, its dominance did not prevent the rise of a continuing partisan alignment for civil rights. A second is that this dominance did not impose a parallel structure, much less a parallel trajectory, on the alignment of rights preferences. Finally and most crucially for Chapter 3, the rise of two lasting partisan alignments did not prevent the rise of additional alignments based on different policy substances with different social roots.

Economic crisis had propelled social welfare to the center of American politics, where the continuing presence of class interests sustained the resulting alignment into our time. The rise of civil rights was more the response to a conscious "rights revolution," whose crucial product was the deliberate reform of voter enfranchisement, leading to a veritable reconstitution of the electoral base for American politics. Yet if there was room for further policy domains and additional social cleavages to shape the enduring alignments characterizing this politics, there could also be additional engines of change (and then sustenance) driving any such possibility. In fact, most accounts of the evolution of postwar American politics found themselves forced to attend to just such a third policy domain, namely cultural values; to a third associated cleavage, namely religious denomination; and to a third change engine, namely *partisan mobilization*.

The Social Roots of American Politics. Regina L. Wagner and Byron E. Shafer, Oxford University Press.
© Oxford University Press 2022. DOI: 10.1093/oso/9780197650844.003.0004

The latter is the process whereby (1) established social cleavages acquire new substantive implications, (2) altered implications necessitate new party attachments, and (3) the resultant (re)alignments are driven thereafter by interactions among, as well as the simple growth or decline of, the social groups whose policy preferences set off the initial causal chain—in a search for more and better reflection of policy preferences by the political parties. Less abstractly, with partisan mobilization as their particular engine, it was cultural issues that would come to challenge both social welfare and civil rights at various times after the Second World War, managing to dominate them on occasion while causing many analysts to think of culture-crossed-with-economics as the joint axes of policy conflict in modern American politics.[1]

Macro-arguments aside, these cultural conflicts did come to be more or less intrinsically connected to their dominant social cleavage in the form of major religious denominations, which had long been the conventional seedbeds for public thinking about social norms and the good society.[2] There was no inescapable crisis driving their ascendancy, certainly not on the scale of the Great Depression. There was no deliberate reform underpinning this rise, as there clearly was with voter enfranchisement. Yet the emergent links among policy preferences, social cleavages, and party attachments would be sufficient to set off a major, more or less accidental, partisan mobilization in the domain of cultural values—accidental, that is, until party operatives began to focus on it, working consciously to secure all the stereotypical further effects.

The Search for a Cultural Alignment

There was little to suggest this possibility in the early postwar years. Extension of the welfare state, pursuit of an international "cold war," and the rise of civil rights were all intrusively on the national agenda. Cultural issues were not, to the point where if there was a dominant theme to cultural commentary in the 1950s, it involved an apparent desire for social peace, shared values, and "normalcy."[3] This is not to say that conflicts over these issues had not bulked large in American politics at a variety of historical moments. Some of the original colonies were, after all, denominational products, and there had been a "great awakening" of religious fervor in the early years of the new nation.[4] Even more explicitly, cultural conflicts over everything from the proper choice of Bibles to the proper hours for alcohol consumption were central to the years after the Civil War, before the Great Depression drove them off center stage.[5]

Evidently, then, the practical priority of cultural issues could both rise and fall, though when they had been on the rise, the social cleavage associated with their policy divisions was clear enough. One or another aspect of denominational attachment—the churched versus the un-churched, Catholics versus Protestants, or the great split within Protestantism between Mainlines and Evangelicals—had provided the social divisions underpinning earlier policy disputes. Yet absent forty years of foresight, there was little to discern by way of a focus either on cultural values from one side or on denominational families from the other during the immediate postwar years. A look backward through the same data that picked up welfare divisions from the start and rights divisions shortly thereafter produces little that would suggest that a picture of cultural quiescence was inaccurate in its time.

Social preconditions were certainly present. American society was religiously diverse, with four great denominational families: Mainline Protestants, Evangelical Protestants, Catholics, and Others.[6] So doctrinal differences by denomination could have been central to political coalitions, had cultural values been central to public preferences (Table 3.1.A). Inside this hypothetical result, the two great plurality blocs were the Mainline Protestants and the Catholics. Closely balanced in size, the two together did constitute a statistical majority. Yet seen another way, one more common to summaries of the time, what was implicit instead was a "Protestant nation," with the Mainlines plus the Evangelicals possessing an alternative statistical majority.[7] Yet the point here is that party politics in the early postwar years was to repress rather than express all such coalitional possibilities.

Mainline Protestants were majority Republican, tipping them in one partisan direction, while Catholics were overwhelmingly Democratic, tipping them

Table 3.1 **A Denominational Picture of American Society, 1950–1970**

A. Denominational Shares		B. Denominations by Party	
MP	37%	MP	55% Rep, 45% Dem
EP	19%	EP	30% Rep, 70% Dem
C	35%	C	26% Rep, 74% Dem
O	9%	O	22% Rep, 78% Dem

C. By Denominations within Parties

1. Republicans		2. Democrats	
MP	54%	MP	26%
EP	16%	EP	21%
C	25%	C	42%
O	5%	O	11%

strongly the other way (Table 3.1.B). Had cultural issues been sufficient to align the two branches of Protestantism, the Republican Party would have been well on the way to becoming the political church of a putative Protestant nation.[8] Yet Evangelicals were heavily Democratic; Catholics were a larger share of the Democratic Party than either Protestant family; and the Others, that is, non-Christians and the nonidentified, were solidly Democratic as well (Table 3.1.C). So if cultural values had been consequential and denominational attachments had been activated, the existing Democratic coalition would have been particularly difficult to manage, containing as it did the two theological extremes, the Evangelicals and the Others, along with a Catholic plurality with which both were neither theologically nor behaviorally comfortable.[9]

Potential influence for this denominational structure was further constrained by the simple lack of much connection between public preferences on cultural values and either party attachment or denominational family. By party, Democrats were modestly left of the national average on culture and Republicans modestly right of it, a trivial difference by comparison to the ideological gulf between Democrats and Republicans on social welfare or even civil rights, and thus one that immediately risked being an artifact of some third influence (Table 3.2.A). By denomination, the three statistically consequential families sat very close to the national average (and hence to each other) when culture was

Table 3.2 **Party Attachment, Religious Denomination, and Policy Preference: Cultural Values, 1950–1970**

A. By Party		B. By Denomination	
All Dems	−.03	Evangelical Prots (EP)	+.06
All Reps	+.04	Mainline Prots (MP)	+.01
		Catholics (C)	+.00
		Others (O)	−.29

C. By Denominations within Parties	
O Dem	−.36
O Rep	−.14
MP Dem	−.08
C Dem	+.01
C Rep	+.01
EP Dem	+.06
EP Rep	+.08
MP Rep	+.09

Cultural Values and Religious Denominations

the focus, while a further look at region will make it clear that the ever-so-modestly greater conservatism of the Evangelical Protestants was a product of geography and not religion affiliation[10] (Table 3.2.B).

A hint of suppressed priority for denomination did appear when the four great religious families were cut into partisan pieces, that is, by denominations within parties (Table 3.2.C). Seen this way, the two partisan pieces of the Others contributed the obvious liberal end of the cultural spectrum. The two pieces of Evangelical Protestantism contributed a much more modest conservative end. And the two partisan pieces of American Catholicism fell in the center of this array, essentially on the national average. Yet this incipient organization was immediately jumbled by the fact that it did not reach into the largest denomination. Mainline Protestantism deviated from the clustering typical of the other religious families by offering partisan pieces that sat on opposite sides of the national average, a dissident alignment in these opening postwar years but one destined to acquire larger implications over time.

That was the old world of religious potential for political influence in the nation as a whole. Yet as with civil rights, though in a very different way, this national picture masked a further, major, regional disjunction, one that would more or less eradicate any denominational contribution to policy alignment on cultural values in these early years. To begin with, the two regions were very different denominational worlds (Table 3.3.A and B). Catholicism was the plurality in the North, Evangelicalism was the plurality in the South, while the plurality in the nation as a whole, Mainstream Protestantism, was not the leading denomination in either great geographic region. This distribution was enough to cause some analysts at the time to think of the two great regions as distinct cultural worlds.[11]

Yet when party was crossed with denomination inside this regional divide, denomination as a direct shaping influence on policy alignments more or less disappeared. With party attachment, the ideological continuum for what were now four regional parties looked very much like the counterpart alignment for civil rights in the immediate postwar years, running left to right from Northern

Table 3.3 **Religious Denominations by Geographic Region, 1950–1970**

	A. North	*B. South*
MP	36%	38%
EP	11%	47%
C	42%	10%
O	10%	5%

Democrats to Northern Republicans to Southern Democrats to Southern Republicans (Table 3.4.A). Yet unlike civil rights, this cultural continuum featured roughly equal contributions from party and from region. Democrats and Republicans were about the same distance apart in the North and in the South, while the North and the South were about the same distance apart among Democrats and Republicans.

So joint consideration of party and region more or less demolished any further influence for denominational membership (Table 3.4.B). The modest initial twist on cultural preferences by denomination that appeared when religion was considered by itself proved to be overwhelmingly a regional artifact. Only two of the four great religious families, the Mainstreams and the Evangelicals, had a serious statistical presence in the South. Catholics were highly concentrated in a very few places, while the Others were scarce everywhere. But the two families that did have a serious presence in both the North and the South were essentially indistinguishable *within* regions, implying that region, not denomination, was responsible for creating an apparent ideological difference between the two.

Put back together, then, party attachment, social cleavage, and geographic region—the three potential organizing devices for the three policy domains analyzed so far—assumed a different order in each (Table 3.5). With social welfare, party was dominant, supported by social class, with region bringing up the rear. For civil rights, race was strongest, with region retaining a powerful

Table 3.4 **Party Attachment, Religious Denomination, and Policy Preference: Cultural Values by Geographic Region, 1950–1970**

A. By Party			B. By Denomination		
	1. North	*2. South*		*1. North*	*2. South*
Dems	−.09	+.08	MP	−.02	+.15
Reps	+.03	+.21	EP	−.03	+.15
			C	+.00	[+.06]
			O	−.32	[−.27]
			[Very small N]		

Table 3.5 **Organizing Principles for Policy Alignment by Domain, 1950–1970**

	Social Welfare	*Civil Rights*	*Cultural Values*
Primary	Party	Race	Region
Secondary	Class	Region	Party
Tertiary	Region	Party	Denomination

role inside the racial majority, while party contributed least to an overall alignment. For cultural values, finally, region was the dominant influence, followed by party—parties did show up *within* regions—with denomination effectively neutralized by the regional divide. The religious families were distributed differently between the regions, which surely gave cultural aspects of their societies a different character. But when policy preferences on cultural values were the focus, region in effect neutralized denominational membership.

The Belated Appearance of a Partisan Alignment

Social welfare had produced a fully articulated partisan alignment in the opening postwar period, linking social class and welfare preferences with party attachment, then expanding this arrangement in the successor era. Civil rights had offered only a weak, ambiguous, and contingent parallel in the opening period, with party attachment still dominated by both racial background and geographic region, before coming into a common alignment with social welfare in the successor era. Yet cultural values lacked even the weak partisan echo that had characterized civil rights in the opening era, featuring only a cross-cutting jumble of party, denomination, and region. Moreover, the same measures in the successor era would largely repeat the same jumble.

So it would be the modern era before cultural values joined the partisan alignment by then characterizing the other three policy domains, though when it did, it would arrive in explosive fashion. Before that, the central story of the second postwar period was stasis, apparently confirming a fundamental difference between cultural values and the other domains and suggesting not the reorganization of a comprehensive alignment but only the instantiation of previously jumbled patterns. With hindsight, however, we can know that a comprehensive realignment was coming, and it is even possible to recognize individual harbingers of the collective change that would ultimately produce a very different overall alignment.

As ever, a partisan alignment common to the other three domains had to become visible through a focus on party attachment, previously overshadowed by both geographic region and religious denomination in the cultural domain. But party attachment was to shape a new cultural alignment in a distinctive manner, one diagnostic of a third—entirely different—engine of political change. In the aggregate, the central social cleavage, religious denomination, was to remain roughly stable within this major shift. Unlike both class and race, it was not to be a direct influence on an emerging partisan alignment. Instead, change would come through the infusion of party attachment *inside* each of the four great religious families, where it had been more or less absent in previous years.

Table 3.6 Party Attachment and Policy Alignment: Cultural Values across the Postwar Period

	A. By Party		B. By Denomination				
	Dems	Reps	MP	EP	C	O	
Era 3	−.16	+.22	0	+.15	−.04	−.26	Era 3
Era 2	−.06	+.07	−.02	+.13	+.03	−.36	Era 2
Era 1	−.03	+.04	+.02	+.07	+.01	−.30	Era 1

C. By Denominations within Parties

1. Dems				2. Reps				
MP	EP	C	O	MP	EP	C	O	
Era 3	−.20	−.02	−.14	−.40	+.18	+.38	+.11	+.04	Era 3
Era 2	−.09	+.08	−.01	−.46	+.02	+.21	+.09	−.16	Era 2
Era 1	−.09	+.06	+.01	−.36	+.09	+.08	+.01	−.14	Era 1

Cultural values did offer a slightly greater ideological distinction between the two parties in the second postwar period (Table 3.6.A). Yet this partisan polarization was mild enough that it could have resulted from little more than random motion; it was certainly not the evident catalyst for an altered evolutionary trajectory. Indeed, in comparative terms, cultural values actually fell behind—it now lagged—all three other major domains. By this second postwar period, the partisan gap on social welfare had grown to nearly four times that on cultural values. The counterpart gap on civil rights was nearly three times that on cultural values. And national security, the one domain even more weakly aligned by party in the opening period (and a central element in Chapter 4), had come into full partisan alignment, now twice as polarized by party as cultural values.

Yet in the modern era, this old world would finally be upended. Cultural values as a policy domain was to assume an ideological divide, leaving little doubt that a true partisan alignment had arrived, with party attachment as the critical marker. If this domain remained the least polarized of the four majors, its modern change would nevertheless represent a tripling of the polarization previously characterizing cultural values, by far the largest of four polarizing moves in the modern era. So the natural next question, emphasized by the way that policy alignments on cultural values had previously been the most resistant to partisan (re)shaping, was where this new move had come from. Surprisingly, especially by comparison to social welfare or civil rights, it had not come directly out of the relevant social cleavage, namely religious denomination.

Instead, realignment came from the *interaction* of denomination and party, through a process known as partisan mobilization. In the second postwar period, denominational membership had offered only a grab-bag of small changes specific to the individual denominations (Table 3.6.B). The largest moves came among the Evangelicals and the Others, but in truth, comparable movements were not all that different inside the other two.[12] Far more striking was the fact that ideological movement by aggregate denomination remained small, nearly trivial, into the modern era. The four major religious families continued to show the same ideological order that they had presented in the immediate postwar years, while the ideological gap between the most liberal and the most conservative, never approaching that for racial background or social class, actually declined from the second to the third postwar eras.

So what *had* driven a dramatic new alignment on cultural values for the modern era? The answer lay in what was happening inside the four denominational families. In fact, all four ingested a strong dose of partisan polarization *by denomination* (Table 3.6.C). If these religious families as individual aggregates continued to stand in roughly the same locations that they had always offered, the divides internal to each expanded hugely. It was these *four* ideological gaps, within denominations and not across them, that added up to a sharply augmented alignment by party for the nation as a whole.[13] The gap between party identifiers inside Mainstream Protestantism went from .07 to .38, inside Evangelical Protestantism from. 02 to .40, inside Catholicism from .00 to .25, and among the Others from .22 to .44.

For the individual Democratic pieces, their ideological ordering remained as it had been in the beginning, and the same could be said of the individual Republican pieces. But that was only additional testimony to the power of partisan polarization *inside* each denomination. A further result was that every Democratic denominational piece was now liberal and every Republican piece conservative, likewise untrue in both preceding periods and yet another measure of the seismic shift in policy alignments on cultural values. If the ideological ordering among the big four denominations remained stable while a partisan infusion exploded inside each, however, the overall contribution of this partisan mobilization to a new and overarching cultural alignment was further augmented by patterns of growth and decline among the big four.

The two growth populations were the Evangelicals and the Others, the ideological extremes among the four great families (Table 3.7.A). The two declining populations were the Mainstreams and the Catholics, the two reliably centrist families. The Evangelicals enjoyed major growth across both successor periods after the immediate postwar years, while the Others experienced their growth spurt in the modern era. Conversely, major Catholic losses were concentrated in the second postwar period while stabilizing in the modern world, when the

THE SOCIAL ROOTS OF AMERICAN POLITICS

Table 3.7 **Augmenting the Power of Partisan Mobilization: Denominational Growth and Decline**

A. In the Electorate

	Era 1	Era 2	Era 3
MP	37%	37%	23%
EP	19%	27%	36%
C	35%	27%	25%
O	9%	9%	16%

B. In the Parties

	Dems			Reps			
	Era 1	Era 2	Era 3	Era 1	Era 2	Era 3	
MP	26%	29%	19%	54%	48%	28%	MP
EP	21%	30%	36%	16%	24%	37%	EP
C	42%	30%	26%	25%	22%	24%	C
O	11%	11%	19%	5%	7%	11%	O

Mainstreams suffered their huge contraction. So these trends contributed further twists to a major mobilization by party that came home to roost in the modern era. Yet that was not the end even of this demographic story, since growth or decline was experienced in different fashions inside the two parties.

Neither escaped the overall changes: Evangelicals and Others up, Catholics and Mainstreams down. But common growth and decline were still experienced very differently by party (Table 3.7.B). The Mainstreams declined inside both parties in the modern era, but the decline was dramatic inside the Republican Party, where they lost their plurality status. The Evangelicals grew inside both parties in the second as well as the third periods, but this growth was explosive among the Republicans. Catholics declined in the second period within both parties, but almost all of the proportionate loss came among the Democrats, while Catholic Republicans were roughly stable as a share of their partisan home. And the Others grew vigorously inside both, especially in the modern era, though that left them as a considerably more serious part of the Democratic Party.[14]

The four major partisan populations provide a different but essentially parallel route into this evolutionary story. The four had begun by suggesting that policy alignments for cultural values were different in kind from the other domains, and this difference, whatever it was, continued into the successor period (Table 3.8). By that time, the two rank-and-file populations had diverged

Cultural Values and Religious Denominations

Table 3.8 **Policy Preferences by Partisan Population: Cultural Values across the Postwar Period**

	DAcs	DRFs	RRFs	RAcs	
Era 3	−.30	−.13	+.21	+.28	Era 3
Era 2	−.23	−.02	+.09	+.01	Era 2
Era 1	−.08	−.04	+.07	+.02	Era 1

in their policy preferences by party in the three other domains, where their activists went on to stake out additionally extreme positions. Yet on cultural values, from the start and continuing in this successor era, activists had created an evidently different ideological *order*, both sitting to the left of their rank and files inside their respective parties.

By itself, this dissident alignment was little more than another idiosyncrasy in a domain that lacked a dominant organizing principle. Yet that did not necessarily make a dissident alignment into an empirical anomaly. Rather, it appeared to embody a major aspect of applied democratic theory, one implicitly arguing that cultural values *ought* to feature a different ordering. In this view, cultural values captured not just social traditionalism versus social progressivism but also—and perhaps especially in an era when specific concerns about cultural policy were not on the front of the public brain—a basic orientation toward democratic norms. Seen this way, either political activism attracted individuals who already supported these norms or augmented participation taught active individuals their importance.[15]

Either way, party activists, Democratic or Republican, ought to be inherently more supportive than their rank and files of the aspects of cultural values that involved civil liberties. So it was reasonable to suggest that just such an alignment had surfaced in the first postwar period, was carried over into the second period, and therefore had to be demolished in the third in order to come into a common alignment with the three other policy domains. By the third postwar period, it would be obvious that partisan mobilization was capable of producing the necessary demolition. Yet as with many other elements of cultural politics, there had been individual moves among specific partisan populations that would prove by hindsight to have been harbingers of this modern demolition.

If the dominant public theme of the immediate postwar years had been cultural quiescence, then the dominant public theme of its successor period became cultural upheaval. Widespread demonstrations and protests embodied values that were gathered by aspiring spokesmen into what they called a "counter-culture," intended to underline divisions, not commonality, in American life.[16] American National Election Study (ANES) data pick up no serious impact on mass partisan alignment in this immediate period, suggesting either that the alleged counterculture was more of a focus for its attentive audience than for the general public or that, coming after a period of cultural quiescence, such a divide could not immediately generate a fully articulated alignment.[17] Yet among the individual partisan populations, there were developments related to this nascent cultural divide that would bear precisely this fruit in the modern era.

Democratic activists were the population most attracted to the extremely liberal preferences associated with a consciously divisive cultural movement. In response, the active Democratic Party dove off to the left on cultural values during the second postwar period. At the time, this move was clearly idiosyncratic, that is, unshared with any other partisan population. Nevertheless, it was sufficient to take these activists so far from their own rank and file that the vast bulk of the Democratic Party was not only closer to the Republican rank and file but also better represented by Republican activists. The Democratic rank and file would remain the most culturally moderate of the four partisan populations, though even it was to move away from the national average in the modern era, while its activists would continue—in effect, lock in—a clear leftward drift.

The auspicious contrary development, if contemporaries had only known, was the continuing cultural moderation of the active Republican Party, a moderation underlined by the fact that Republican activists continued to sit clearly left of their own rank and file. Patently, that rank and file was not attracted by a new liberalism on cultural policy, as it edged ever so slightly to the cultural right in this second period. In so doing, it provided another example of a rank and file that was out ahead of its activists in terms of policy change,[18] though Republican activists would more than catch up in the modern era, when they made the biggest ideological shift of the four populations, diving sharply off to the right. That move completed the realignment of cultural values, while simultaneously annulling an older argument that this domain captured procedural norms rather than policy preferences.[19]

Regions in a Polarizing Nation

Cultural values was initially distinguished as the policy domain most clearly organized not by party attachment or by social cleavage but by geographic region. That alone would make it essential to revisit region within culture for subsequent periods. The eventual arrival of a comprehensive partisan alignment nationwide did imply that party attachment, on the rise as an organizing principle, had to be constraining the influence of geographic region on cultural values. Yet a regionally diverse beginning and a nationally common finish almost required that the individual regions evolve in different manners, while leaving open the possibility that a national alignment could still be composed of regional counterparts that differed notably but still added up to that national alignment.

Demographic change alone would feature major regional differences. Mainstream Protestantism was already in decline by the second era in the South but not yet the North, and while a decline would characterize both regions in the modern era, this decline was to become huge in the North this time (Table 3.9.A). Evangelicalism maintained an unshaken dominance in the South while adding a galloping increase in the North, where it moved from a tangential religious choice to a competitor for denominational leadership. The decline of

Table 3.9 Augmenting the Power of Partisan Mobilization: Denominational Growth and Decline by Region

A. In the Electorate

	1. North			2. South			
	Era 1	Era 2	Era 3	Era 1	Era 2	Era 3	
MP	36%	39%	24%	38%	30%	21%	MP
EP	11%	17%	27%	47%	50%	52%	EP
C	42%	30%	31%	10%	15%	16%	C
O	10%	14%	18%	5%	5%	11%	O

B. In the Parties

	1. North						
	Dems			Reps			
	Era 1	Era 2	Era 3	Era 1	Era 2	Era 3	
MP	22%	25%	17%	45%	43%	26%	MP
EP	26%	34%	39%	17%	26%	38%	EP
C	39%	28%	24%	31%	23%	24%	C
O	13%	13%	20%	7%	8%	12%	O

	2. South						
	Dems			Reps			
	Era 1	Era 2	Era 3	Era 1	Era 2	Era 3	
MP	32%	35%	17%	56%	40%	27%	MP
EP	52%	53%	55%	31%	43%	47%	EP
C	11%	17%	16%	8%	12%	17%	C
O	5%	5%	12%	5%	5%	9%	O

Catholicism was concentrated in the North and in the second period, though in the South, where it was always a relatively uncommon religious preference, it actually rose. And the Others were on a consistent rise in the North across both periods, with a Southern surge coming only in the modern era and leaving them a comparatively lesser religious choice.

Yet demographic change would have further directly partisan effects inside this regional evolution. The decline in Mainstream Protestantism became most consequential among Southern Republicans and least consequential among Northern Democrats (Table 3.9.B). Conversely, the rise of Evangelical Protestantism contributed the most to Northern Republicans and the least to Southern Democrats. A decline of Catholicism that hit hardest among Northern Democrats made its largest positive contribution to Southern Republicans. And a rise by the Others nationwide still left them strongest among Northern Democrats and weakest among Southern Republicans.

The overall national story otherwise featured only idiosyncratic shifts from the first to the second postwar period, a few of which would be harbingers of the modern era, most of which suggested temporal stability rather than looming transformation. And the same could be said of the evolutionary contribution of the two regions. In the immediate postwar years, geographic region had overwhelmed party attachment as an organizing principle for cultural values (Table 3.10.A). Democrats were left of Republicans in both major regions, but the ideological continuum placed both Northern parties to the left of both Southern counterparts. The second postwar period was nearly a direct copy of the first, apart from one regional twist: the gap between Democrats and Republicans in their cultural preferences actually declined in the South, reducing the influence of party and thus making region even more dominant there.

Yet the third postwar period was to register the comprehensive demise of this old cultural order. Partisan polarization was on the rise everywhere, not just nationally but also in the regions. In the North, the distance between Democrats and Republicans tripled. In the South, it quintupled. Collectively, these changes were substantial enough to foster an advancing regional convergence, where the propensity of Southern Democrats to sit to the right of Northern Republicans finally disappeared. What was left of the old regional dominance was just the way that each regional party remained more conservative in the South than in the North, though even this difference became trivial among Republicans, remaining substantial only among the Democrats: Southern Democrats still stood out on cultural values.

Where had these collective changes come from? For the nation as a whole, the answer was a wide-ranging and explosive process of partisan mobilization. The great religious families as aggregates did not change their policy preferences, but their internal partisan pieces—their Democratic versus Republican

Table 3.10 Geographic Region and Policy Preferences: Cultural Values across the Postwar Period

A. By Party

	1. North		2. South		
	Dems	Reps	Dems	Reps	
Era 3	−.23	+.19	−.06	+.26	Era 3
Era 2	−.13	+.04	+.08	+.14	Era 2
Era 1	−.07	+.02	+.08	+.17	Era 1

B. By Denominations within Parties

1. North

	Dems				Reps				
	MP	EP	C	O	MP	EP	C	O	
Era 3	−.22	−.12	−.15	−.44	+.16	+.37	+.11	+.07	Era 3
Era 2	−.15	−.03	−.02	−.45	+.01	+.18	+.08	−.18	Era 2
Era 1	−.14	−.05	+.01	−.36	+.07	+.03	0	−.17	Era 1

2. South

	Dems				Reps				
	MP	EP	C	O	MP	EP	C	O	
Era 3	−.18	+.05	−.12	−.32	+.22	+.39	+.10	+.04	Era 3
Era 2	+.02	+.15	+.07	−.37	+.09	+.23	+.13	−.14	Era 2
Era 1	+.10	+.12	+.04	−.35	+.22	+.24	*	*	Era 1

* N too small for statistical reliability.

identifiers—opened a large ideological gap inside all four denominations. The same story, that is, a rise in the power of party attachment, by way of four individually polarizing denominations, could once more be generalized to the regions. The North and the South did begin in ideologically different territory, so the South had to move more than the North on the way to a greater commonality. Yet their overall trajectories were to remain roughly parallel.

The North began as more liberal than the South in every denomination, a testament to the greater organizing power of region over party (Table 3.10.B.1). The North then moved nearly not at all in the successor period, with one noteworthy exception: Northern Republican Evangelicals—in one of those hindsight harbingers—moved clearly to the right. A Northern regional move into the modern era then extended this incipient partisan mobilization among Evangelicals to every denomination. The ideological gap between party identifiers among Mainstreams went from .16 to .38, among Evangelicals from .21 to .49, among Catholics from .10 to .26, and among the Others from .27 to .52.

The South began as uniformly more conservative, though there were not enough Catholics or Others among its Republicans to register their preferences reliably (Table 3.10.B.2). The successor period did see the appearance of measurable Catholics and Others. Yet what would prove more politically consequential for a Southern alignment was the lack of ideological motion in this second era, a stasis that would make the generalized partisan mobilization of the modern era look even more striking.[20] In this third postwar period, the gap between Mainstreams in the South went from .06 to .40, among Evangelicals from .08 to .34, among Catholics from .06 to .22, and among Others from .23 to .36.

In the North, the ideological distance between partisan pieces of the four denominations essentially doubled in the modern era. In the South, it essentially quadrupled, drawing the regions toward convergence while augmenting the power of party attachment. An increasingly common alignment more or less automatically reduced the organizing power of region, while the denominations continued to stand in the same ideological order, inside both parties and for both regions. Within this ordering, the Others sustained their comparative liberalism, though their Republican pieces finally became conservative in both regions for the modern era.[21] The Evangelicals continued their comparative conservatism, while Southern Evangelical Democrats did not become liberal even in this modern world.

In other words, stray indications of a partisan mobilization in the second postwar period became a realigning explosion in the modern era. In the process, the triumph of party attachment over geographic region underlined the power of partisan mobilization as a change engine. In principle, this dynamic was available to any policy domain and any social cleavage; it will surface less dramatically with national security and sex in the next chapter.[22] But partisan mobilization was most integral to the evolution of a cultural alignment, so the critical theater for this mobilization process had to involve the social cleavage that was most clearly connected to this policy domain too, namely religious denomination.

What all this implied still needs to be summarized with care. A common partisan alignment now united cultural values with social welfare, civil rights, and (as we shall see) national security. Inside the cultural version, party attachment had finally overtaken geographic region as an aligning influence. Yet the result was shaped most critically by the exploding role of party attachment *inside* denominational membership. So the interaction of religious denomination and party attachment was what remained truly critical to a new partisan alignment on cultural values. Region was a collateral casualty, though vestigial impacts did

Cultural Values and Religious Denominations 81

remain, more than marginal only between the regional Democratic Parties and most especially their Evangelical Protestant adherents.

A Fifth Denomination?

The logic of partisan alignment as an analytic device—as a tool for investigating links among policy preferences, social cleavages, and party attachments—strongly counsels treating the four great religious families in the manner presented to this point in Chapter 3.[23] Yet unlike the other major social cleavages, religious denomination has a substantial subset of scholarly students who favor an alternative approach, arguing that such an analysis should recognize a fifth great family. Working from doctrinal differences within Evangelical Protestantism while drawing on the differential distribution of black and nonblack Americans among religious families, these scholars propose that black Evangelicals be separated from their nonblack brethren and carried as an independent category.[24]

This alternative approach presents serious theoretical difficulties for an exercise like this one: group-specific concerns are not theological positions, and racial backgrounds are not religious denominations.[25] Still, these arguments raise the possibility of an analytic categorization that might be empirically important to partisan alignments, and nowhere more than on cultural values. Fortunately, the empirical impact of an adjusted religious taxonomy is easy to test. Step one is to stratify black Americans by religious denomination. Step two is to stratify religious denominations by racial background. And step three is to take the result, if intellectually provocative, and use it to recast key prior exhibits, especially the ones underlining the power of partisan mobilization as a change engine.

Black Americans do in fact offer disproportionate loyalty to Evangelical Protestantism, while allocating little more than statistical remnants to the other three religious families (Table 3.11.A). Conversely, black Americans constitute an important part of the Evangelical population but only a residual portion of the

Table 3.11 **A Fifth Denomination? Religious Denominations by Racial Background**

A. Among Blacks		B. By Race		
EP	77%	EP	67% Wh,	33% Bl
MP	10%	MP	94% Wh,	6% Bl
C	6%	C	96% Wh,	4% Bl
O	7%	O	93% Wh,	7% Bl

other three (Table 3.11.B). So the question of an appropriate denominational classification boils down to what can be said about racial divisions on cultural values within Evangelical Protestantism.[26] Two summary answers emerge. From their side, black Evangelicals evince little interest in cultural conflicts across the entire postwar period. From the other side, Protestant Evangelicalism, already the denominational pivot for cultural values during this extended period, looks additionally distinctive minus its black adherents, and thus even more central to the impact of partisan mobilization.

Table 3.12 carves out the black Evangelicals (BE) and subtracts them from the previous Evangelical population [EP1], creating a revised nonblack Evangelical Protestantism (EP). As a separate denomination sitting close to the national average in the immediate postwar years, black Evangelicals would more or less stay there across all the years to come. In this aggregate denominational sense, they were little different from the Mainstream Protestants or the

Table 3.12 **Religious Denomination and Policy Preference Revisited: Cultural Values across the Postwar Period**

A. By Denomination

	MP	EP	[EP1]	C	O	BE	
Era 3	0	+.24	[+.16]	−.04	−.26	−.04	Era 3
Era 2	−.02	+.18	[+.13]	+.03	−.36	+.01	Era 2
Era 1	+.02	+.08	[+.07]	+.01	−.30	−.04	Era 1

EP1: Evangelical Protestantism as a composite of EP and BE

B. By Denominations within Parties

	1. Dems					
	MP	EP	[EP1]	C	O	BE
Era 3	−.20	+.01	[−.02]	−.14	−.40	−.05
Era 2	−.09	+.15	[+.08]	−.01	−.46	−.01
Era 1	−.08	+.06	[+.06]	+.01	−.36	−.02

	2. Reps					
	MP	EP	[EP1]	C	O	BE
Era 3	+.18	+.39	[+.38]	+.11	+.04	*
Era 2	+.02	+.21	[+.21]	+.09	−.16	*
Era 1	+.09	+.08	{+.08]	+.01	−.14	*

* N too small for statistical reliability.

Catholics, and clearly different from the Others and the redefined Evangelicals. These Others were always the ideologically extreme denominational family, just as the redefined Evangelicals continued to be the ones making the biggest ideological move across the postwar period.

Yet the introduction of stratification by party within denomination was what revealed the true—and much more explosive—impact of denominational membership. Said the other way around, partisan mobilization was the mechanism bringing a comprehensive partisan alignment to cultural values, while making each of its denominational pieces look additionally distinctive (Table 3.12.B). For black Evangelicals, however, the mechanism was irrelevant. There was never a serious Republican piece to this denomination. Moreover, compared to the other eight denominational pieces created by party attachment, black Evangelicals were the true centrists, the denominational piece closest to the national average for the postwar period as a whole.

Beyond that, the statistical impact from isolating black Evangelicals was to be found in the impact of this separation on the cultural preferences of a redefined Evangelicalism, where the partisan divide still had substantial consequences. Absent black Evangelicals, this redefined Evangelicalism already showed a greater conservatism on cultural values by the second postwar period, though at that point, Democratic as well as Republican Evangelicals were moving clearly to the right. So only in the modern era did partisan mobilization invade a redefined Evangelicalism in a major way. In this third postwar period, Republican Evangelicals produced an even stronger move to the right on cultural policy. Yet this time, Democratic Evangelicals produced a solid move to the left, and if this still did not make them liberals, it did expand the partisan division within Evangelicalism.[27]

On the one hand, the two partisan pieces of Protestant Evangelicalism, that is, Evangelical Democrats versus Evangelical Republicans, were about the same distance apart as the partisan pieces of the other denominations. In that sense, party attachment had overcome both religious denomination and racial background. On the other hand, this still understates the expanding role of Evangelical Protestantism in postwar partisan alignments, because it ignores the fact that both Evangelical branches were growing, albeit on an increasingly different scale as between the two parties.

The huge growth of a composite Evangelical population did result from growth among both Evangelical branches (Table 3.13.A). Black Evangelicals more than doubled their share of the American electorate, though it comes as no surprise that their presence nearly tripled among Democratic identifiers, while remaining at less than 1% of the Republican Party (Table 3.13.B). With black Evangelicals treated as a separate religious category, the growth of a redefined Evangelicalism does look less dramatic. Yet nonblack Evangelicals

Table 3.13 **Growth and Decline Revisited**

A. In the Electorate

	Era 1	Era 2	Era 3
MP	37%	37%	23%
EP	19%	27%	36%
C	35%	27%	25%
O	9%	9%	16%
BE	5%	7%	12%

B. In the Parties

	Dems			Reps			
	Era 1	Era 2	Era 3	Era 1	Era 2	Era 3	
MP	26%	29%	19%	54%	48%	28%	MP
EP	14%	18%	17%	16%	24%	37%	EP
C	42%	30%	26%	25%	22%	24%	C
O	11%	11%	19%	5%	7%	11%	O
BE	7%	12%	19%	*	*	*	BE

* *N* too small for statistical reliability.

remained a major growth sector in their own right, rising from third among the denominations to an effective tie for first with the two early leaders, the Mainlines and the Catholics (Table 3.13.A). Though this was yet another religious population where party attachment mattered hugely. Among nonblacks, Evangelical Protestants remained a nearly static share of the Democratic Party, becoming ultimately the smallest of five denominations (Table 3.13.B). But inside the Republican Party, Evangelicals went from being a poor third to being the dominant denomination.

Cultural Values, Religious Denominations, and Partisan Alignments

By the modern era, "culture wars"—partisan disputes over cultural policy— would be a recognized feature of American politics.[28] But in the immediate postwar years, this was still a distant development; cultural values sat farther from the center of political conflict than any of the other big-four policy domains. In the aftermath of World War II, social welfare moved back toward the center of this politics, as President Harry Truman sought to "complete" the New Deal, while President Dwight Eisenhower sought a Republican accommodation with it. Civil rights broke through intermittently as a matter of public debate, though not yet insistently as a policy focus. And national security, rather than receding into the political shadows—the traditional response of a historically isolationist nation—experienced comprehensive and continuing policy engagement.

Left out of that picture were policy conflicts driven by cultural values. Social scientists did attend to a posited "American culture."[29] But whatever this was taken to be, it was also taken to be implicit or consensual, or both. And nothing about the policy conflicts that characterized immediate postwar politics would contradict this picture of cultural quiescence. Were cultural issues to move back toward the center of American politics, it was clear enough where their social roots were likely to be. Divisions between the churched and the unchurched, between Protestants and Catholics, or inside Protestantism, pitting Mainstreams against Evangelicals, had all served historically as social cleavages behind public preferences on cultural policy. Moreover, American society continued to present a rich mosaic of all three divides. It was just that they were politically dormant—latent—in those early postwar years.

So there could be nothing approximating the partisan alignment that characterized social welfare from the earliest postwar days and was emerging to characterize civil rights by the successor era. At first blush, there appeared to be a weak counterpart for cultural preferences involving the two major parties plus the four great religious families. But the weak alignment by party was largely a by-product of differential partisan representation for the denominations, while the weak alignment by denomination proved to be almost entirely a product of regional geography. Indeed, unlike the situation for social welfare or civil rights, this very lack of alignment by party attachment or denominational membership was what distinguished cultural values as a policy domain, elevating geographic region as the main organizing influence for its policy alignments.

By hindsight, knowing where all four partisan populations would go, we can see that Democratic activists were diving off to the left on cultural issues in the second postwar period. But in its time, the impact of this shift was largely neutralized by a lesser move in the opposite direction within the (much larger) Democratic rank and file. There were likewise stirrings among Evangelical Protestants, increasingly restive on culture and increasingly drawn toward the Republican Party, but these were modest enough to more or less average out in the total picture. Moreover, Republican activists and their rank and file were moving in opposite directions, liberal for the former and conservative for the latter, making this one of those instances where the rank and file was out ahead of the activists.

86 THE SOCIAL ROOTS OF AMERICAN POLITICS

The modern era was to be very different. Indeed, the break between the first two eras *versus* the third, when measured by partisan alignments, would be striking, in league with the change between partisan alignments on civil rights from the first to the second. What arrived in this modern era was nothing less than a conventional, fully articulated, partisan alignment for cultural values. What produced it was a third great engine of political change, in the form of partisan mobilization. Rather than operating directly, however, partisan mobilization would operate *through* the four great religious families. The partisan pieces of each were to move clearly and strongly away from each other, creating what would become a dominating ideological polarization on cultural issues. Instantiating this partisan polarization, about equally within each major denomination, was what brought that fully articulated partisan alignment into being.[30]

The four great denominations did not change much in their aggregate leanings, with Evangelicals still on the right, the Others still on the left, and Mainstreams plus Catholics still in the middle. Instead, it was a partisan infusion within each—a mobilization of substantive concerns with latent political implications—that drove overall change, though its impact was augmented by the differential growth of the four denominations. The ascendant religious families were the Evangelicals and the Others, the ideological extremes on cultural values. The declining families were the Mainstreams and the Catholics, centrists that had restrained those extremes in earlier eras. Partisan polarization then received a final shove from the fact that Protestant Evangelicals, the most conservative denomination, were disproportionately on the increase within the Republican Party, while the Others, the most liberal denomination, were disproportionately on the increase within its Democratic opposition.

For a long time, the distinctive behavior of party activists in the cultural domain, very different from their behavior with social welfare or civil rights, suggested that the cultural domain was different in kind from these other policy realms. In those domains, the Democratic rank and file stood to the left and the Republican rank and file to the right of the national average, flanked by Democratic activists on the far left and Republican activists on the far right. But for cultural values, activists were instead more liberal than their rank and files inside each party, with Democratic activists left of their rank and file but Republican activists left of theirs as well.

This ordering reinforced the notion that cultural values did, and would naturally, manifest a different policy alignment, reflecting the democratic norms accompanying greater political participation rather than partisan preferences on specifically cultural issues—until the pattern was wiped away in the modern world, to be replaced by the kind of ideological ordering that had characterized social welfare in the first postwar period and civil rights by the second. By then, partisan mobilization was obviously strong enough to pull all four partisan

Cultural Values and Religious Denominations 87

populations into a shared alignment that was characteristic of social welfare or civil rights, and now of cultural values as well.

Coming into the modern era, what had even more clearly distinguished policy alignments on cultural values had been the weakness of party attachment and the strength of geographic region. So geographic region had to suffer a serious decline in its organizing power as both party attachment and denominational membership—now infused by party attachment—rose in their impact. Unlike social welfare or civil rights, however, cultural values was not to see region disappear as an organizing influence. All Southern populations remained marginally to the right of their northern counterparts on cultural values, though the consequential version of this effect was limited to the Democrats, focused by their Southern branch and concentrated on Evangelical Protestants within it.

Where original instantiation and subsequent extension had driven political change on social welfare, and where voter enfranchisement and an altered electorate had driven political change on civil rights, it was partisan mobilization, especially as it interacted with denominational membership, that drove change most centrally on cultural values. Its epicenter was Evangelical Protestantism. Entering the postwar period as only a bit more conservative on cultural matters than either the Mainlines or the Catholics, Evangelical Protestants began to move clearly rightward during the successor period. With hindsight, this was a double move: in bringing partisan politics back to the center of Evangelical life, Protestant Evangelicals were simultaneously bringing cultural values back to the center of partisan politics.[31] Within that development, the main further ideological impetus on cultural values came from those Evangelicals who thought of (or came to think of) themselves as Republicans.

By this third period, Evangelicals had seized leadership on the conservative side of an expanding cultural divide.[32] Yet the way we have handled Protestant Evangelicalism through most of this chapter understates that effect in one key regard. If the analyst were instead to recognize black Evangelicalism as a separate denomination, with theological positions adapted to the social experiences of black Americans, then the move to the cultural right among Evangelicals would have begun earlier and become more conservative for the redefined (nonblack) denomination. Black Evangelicals were effectively uninterested in cultural issues, sitting just left of the national average in every era. So there was a sense in which all this change, impressive as it was and is, was partially masked by the fact that our Evangelical category combined two disparate branches of Evangelical Protestantism.

Either way, treated as one denomination or two, recall that the radically dissident religious family on cultural values had been (and would remain) the collection of Others, a shifting amalgam of Jewish identifiers and those asserting no religious identity. By far the smallest denomination in a period when cultural issues were not high on the policy agenda, their preferences mattered less than they would as cultural issues rose on that national agenda, and especially as these Others became the second growth population of the four denominational families—though in contrast to the Evangelicals in this regard too, their main practical impact on partisan politics would come disproportionately through the Democratic Party.

Members of the two remaining denominations would perforce have to find their place and make their peace with an ideologized and rebalanced religious world. In the early postwar years, the very different party attractions for these two denominations—Mainstreams the leading denomination among Republicans, and Catholics the leading denomination among Democrats—had given each an implicit partisan bias, while giving the parties an incipient sympathy for concerns specific to one or the other denomination. But as cultural values began to redefine partisanship, cultural issues infused these denominations too. For them, however, the story of numerical change was sharply different from that of the Evangelicals or the Others, as Mainstreams and Catholics became the declining denominations among American religious families. When they fell into what were perhaps their inevitable places, however, toward the center of the denominational continuum but every bit as polarized internally as the other denominations, the partisan (re)alignment of cultural values was completed.

‖ 4 ‖

Sex and the Great Reversal in Partisan Alignment

Men, Women, and Policy Preferences

The fourth of what are usually gathered as the four main social cleavages shaping contemporary partisan alignments in the United States is sex, achieving its political impact through the policy preferences distinguishing men from women.[1] The fourth of what are usually conceived as the four major policy domains in American politics since the Second World War, driving and being driven by the links between group membership and policy preference, is national security.[2] That alone would be sufficient reason to bring both into the analysis at this point. Yet at the opening of the postwar period, there was actually something of an expected connection, with men thought to be more conservative (hawkish) and women more liberal (dovish) on national security issues, and this was essentially what showed up in immediate postwar surveys.[3]

That said, however, sex was to prove more variable across policy domains and more labile within them than the other three major cleavages, each of which had an evidently central realm of policy impact: social welfare for social class, civil rights for racial background, and cultural values for religious denomination. By contrast, only one domain, social welfare, would feature alignments by sex that were stable across the full postwar period. In another, civil rights, this relationship would be stable only by virtue of its absence. In a third, cultural values, policy alignments by sex would actually reverse ideological direction. And the fourth, national security, would feature the greatest temporal inconsistency of all, even though it was the lone domain where sex dominated party attachment in the opening period, while resurging to show the strongest connection in the modern era.

So sex could appear, disappear, and rise again as an aligning principle. That suggested either a stable social cleavage whose impact depended on its

---

The Social Roots of American Politics. Regina L. Wagner and Byron E. Shafer, Oxford University Press.
© Oxford University Press 2022. DOI: 10.1093/oso/9780197650844.003.0005

relationship to a shifting menu of policy options of the day or a cleavage that could change its associated policy wishes as the place of sex itself shifted in the larger environment—or, of course, some mix of both. Adding region to this picture would only add variety, with Southern men and women most reliably dissident in the earliest period, most ideologically changeable in the middle period, and most exaggerated in their partisan polarization inside a newly common alignment by the third. So at a minimum, in terms of the central focus of the entire analysis—on the links between a major social cleavage and recurrent policy preferences, as translated crucially by party attachment into ongoing political conflicts—sex was distinct from class, race, or religion.

Yet this kaleidoscope of distinctions, placing men and women in different places in different domains at different periods, would be connected in a much more patterned fashion by yet another—the fourth and final—major engine of political change. Across all the postwar years, the *partisan balance* between men and women was to shift notably and in a linear fashion, with the share of men who were Republicans rising and the share of women who were Democrats rising as well, though the impact among men would be more than twice as large as the countervailing impact among women. So seen the other way around, the changing balance of party identifications tied directly to sex would become the fourth major dynamic (re)shaping partisan alignments in the postwar United States.

Moreover, as a final reflection of the distinctiveness of sex as a social cleavage, this shifting balance would stem from a different *mix* of policy incentives for party switching as between men and women. Opposing preferences in one domain or another, as variable as they would be, were not what would drive partisan rebalancing. Rather, entirely different policy domains were to stimulate distinctive party switches by men versus women. The two sexes might find themselves on different sides of any given policy domain. They might find themselves on the same side, with division created by some cleavage other than sex. Or, and this was what proved decisive, men might be driven to switch parties by preferences in one domain, and women to switch parties by preferences in another.

Initial Links for Sex, Policy, and Party

Results from analysis of the links among social cleavages, policy preferences, and party attachment for the three other great domains of postwar policy conflict—for social welfare by way of social class, for civil rights by way of racial background, and for cultural values by way of religious denomination—have provided a more or less automatic format for pursuing the same analysis in the missing domain,

Men, Women, and Policy Preferences 91

Table 4.1 **Party, Sex, and Policy Preference, 1950–1970**

	A. By Party		B. By Sex	
	Dems	*Reps*	*Women*	*Men*
Social Welfare	−.16	+.24	−.03	+.04
Civil Rights	−.08	+.12	−.03	+.04
Cultural Values	−.03	+.04	+.03	−.04
National Security	−.01	+.02	−.03	+.04

Table 4.2 **Sexes within Parties by Policy Domain, 1950–1970**

A. Domains Aligned by Party over Sex

	Dem Women	*Dem Men*	*Rep Women*	*Rep Men*
Social Welfare	−.18	−.15	+.19	+.30
Civil Rights	−.12	−.03	+.09	+.15

B. Domains Aligned by Party and Sex

	Dem Men	*Dem Women*	*Rep Men*	*Rep Women*
Cultural Values	−.10	+.01	+.02	+.05

C. Domains Aligned by Sex over Party

	Dem Women	*Rep Women*	*Dem Men*	*Rep Men*
National Security	−.06	−.01	+.04	+.05

national security, by way of the missing cleavage, sex. Table 4.1 offers what are now four major domains by the degree to which policy preferences were aligned by party attachment, then by the degree to which those same preferences were aligned by sex. Table 4.2 will add composite links, by sexes within parties, for all four domains.

Three of these stories for the aligning influence of party attachment are familiar (Table 4.1.A). Policy preferences on social welfare were clearly patterned by party from the opening postwar years, with Democrats to the left and Republicans to the right. Policy preferences on civil rights were ordered in the same fashion, but to a much lesser degree. Yet if this relationship was only half as strong as the one with social welfare, it was far stronger than the shadow of a partisan link to cultural values, one that would become indisputable only in the modern era. And national security brought up the rear. In the aggregate, Democrats were left of the national average and Republicans right of it on security issues. But that relationship was so weak that it was every bit as accurate to describe both parties as sitting essentially on the national average.

What kept this final alignment worth noting was its larger, real-world context: this very lack of a partisan divide was appearing in years that were the high point—the "hot" years—of the Cold War.[4] Only hindsight could suggest that a relationship this weak might have reflected not so much partisan irrelevance—perhaps an embodiment of the idea that foreign policy disputes should rightfully stop at the water's edge—but rather a moment of transition in the evolution of security policy.[5] An old world structured by the long struggle between isolationists and internationalists was indeed giving way to a new world structured by hawks and doves in the American-led effort to contain international communism. We shall return to this dynamic later in the chapter.

The same policy preferences stratified by sex showed a different pattern, resulting in different comparative standings for party versus sex as aligning principles (Table 4.1.B). The four alignments by sex produced ideological distances between men and women that were close to identical.[6] Within three of these, namely social welfare, civil rights, and national security, women were the liberals and men the conservatives, though in the fourth, cultural values, those ideologies were reversed, with men liberal and women conservative.[7] Party still trumped sex as an aligning influence in two of these domains, hugely on social welfare and more modestly on civil rights.[8] The two organizing principles were essentially a wash for cultural values. And national security was the one domain where policy differences by sex actually dominated differences by party.

When those two potential organizing principles are considered jointly rather than side by side, that is, as sexes within parties, the overall story changes again. This form of presentation more or less automatically increases the polarizing power of sex, that is, the distance between the farthest left and the farthest right sexualized cohorts, because it doubles the number of cohorts. Yet more consequentially, the major domains no longer placed their four cohorts in even the same ideological order. Social welfare and civil rights aligned the four in a neat and nested pattern (Table 4.2.A). Democrats were left of Republicans in both policy domains, while women were left of men within both parties, an arrangement that testifies to the dominance of party while retaining a further independent influence for sex.

On form, cultural values aligned the four cohorts in the same basic order, but with an important ideological adjustment (Table 4.2.B). Democratic men contributed the left end of the policy continuum this time—the lone left end—while Democratic women, Republican men, and Republican women

Men, Women, and Policy Preferences   93

all clustered modestly to the right of the national average. Finally, the true exception—the only alternative *ordering*—belonged to national security (Table 4.2.C). Here, women were left of men within both parties, while Democrats were left of Republicans within both sexes, an arrangement that testified to the dominance of sex as an organizing principle, while retaining an independent further influence for party.

Yet the great challenge to party attachment as an aligning influence in the first three policy domains, as well as to the social cleavage most relevant to each, was geographic region. So national security needs to be added to the story of regional impacts, while region needs to be added to an analysis of the relationship between sex and policy alignment. Table 4.3 begins this process, featuring the national numbers for each domain, followed by those numbers for the South, normally the dissident region, followed by those numbers for the North—again stratified first by party and then by sex.[9]

From the start, region had been dominated by party on social welfare, the only domain where this was in fact the case (Table 4.3.A.1). Democrats were liberal and Republicans were conservative, while region could distinguish further only among Democrats but not among Republicans. Conversely, region dominated party on both civil rights and cultural values, with a North/South divide that was huge in both cases (Table 4.3.A.2 and 3). Southerners were more conservative than Northerners inside both parties, to such a degree as to disallow any

Table 4.3 **Party, Sex, and Policy Preference in the Regions, 1950–1970**

	A. By Party		**B. By Sex**	
	Dems	*Reps*	*Women*	*Men*
1. Social Welfare	−.16	+.24	−.03	+.03
The South	−.05	+.23	+.04	−.00
The North	−.21	+.24	−.05	+.05
2. Civil Rights	.08	+.12	−.03	+.04
The South	+.16	+.21	+.20	+.16
The North	−.18	+.10	−.10	+.00
3. Cultural Values	−.03	+.04	+.03	−.04
The South	+.06	+.16	+.13	+.04
The North	−.09	+.02	−.02	−.05
4. National Security	−.01	+.02	−.03	+.04
The South	+.03	+.00	+.01	+.04
The North	−.04	+.02	−.07	+.04

regional overlap by party at all—Northern Republicans were more liberal than Southern Democrats. And in the final domain, national security, there was no consistent patterning, to the point where party attachment ran in opposite ideological directions in the North versus the South[10] (Table 4.3.A.4).

So where sex had produced a degree of polarization for policy preferences that was essentially identical across all four domains on the national level, region was to overwhelm this sexual difference in two domains and disarray it in the other two. Civil rights and cultural values were the domains where region simply dominated sex in the same way that it had dominated party: Southerners were again more conservative than Northerners, this time within both sexes[11] (Table 4.3.B.2 and B.3). Region was hardly absent in the other two domains, but it jumbled the links between sex and policy preference in individually distinctive ways. With social welfare, men remained the liberals and women the conservatives in the North, while in the South, they reversed these ideological positions (Table 4.3.B.1). With national security, women continued to be more liberal in the North than in the South, but men assumed nearly identical (moderately conservative) positions in both regions, falling in between Northern and Southern women as they did so (Table 4.3.B.4).

Bringing all of this together through four sexualized partisan alignments was likely to have one of two effects. Either a focus on sexes within parties would provide some overarching parallels to the interaction of policy, party, sex, and region, or this composite focus would reduce an already complex picture to little more than collective idiosyncrasy. On the way to a choice between the two possibilities, Table 4.4 arrays policy preferences in the four major domains by sexes within parties, using the ideological order that characterized social welfare—left to right from Democratic women to Democratic men to Republican women to Republican men—while repeating the ever-present warning that individual domains or separate regions were fully capable of placing their sexualized parties in divergent ideological arrays.

For the nation as a whole, what resulted for social welfare was a richly polarized alignment by party, with a nested alignment by sex inside it (Table 4.4.A, Line 1). What resulted for civil rights was a weaker but parallel alignment (Table 4.4.B, Line 1). What this form of presentation revealed for cultural values was an alignment pitting Democratic men against the three other sexualized parties, offering no patterning apart from the dissidence of Democratic men (Table 4.4.C, Line 1). Finally, what the picture highlighted for national security was an alignment implicitly dissenting from the ordering used to create this table by deviating *in kind*: a more accurate rendering for security policy would have arranged these columns by sex and not by party (Table 4.4.D, Line 1).

But the specific question remains: what role was geographic region playing within these sexualized partisan alignments? In general, the North recapitulated

Men, Women, and Policy Preferences

Table 4.4 **Policy Preferences by Sexes within Parties**

	Dem Women	*Dem Men*	*Rep Women*	*Rep Men*
A. Social Welfare	−.18	−.15	+.19	+.30
The South	−.01	−.06	+.26	+.19
The North	−.24	−.17	+.17	+.32
B. Civil Rights	−.12	−.03	+.09	+.15
The South	+.15	+.18	+.32	+.09
The North	−.26	−.11	+.06	+.13
C. Cultural Values	+.01	−.10	+.05	+.02
The South	+.11	+.01	+.19	+.13
The North	−.01	−.11	+.04	−.00
D. National Security	−.06	+.04	−.01	+.05
The South	+.02	+.09	+.01	+.05
The North	−.10	+.03	−.01	+.05

the national picture, with Democratic men and Democratic women more liberal than their national portrait (Table 4.4.A–D). Conversely, the South was
reliably more conservative than this Northern alignment, with two exceptions.
Southern Republican men, while still conservative, were less conservative than
Northern Republican men on social welfare (Table 4.4.B). And both Southern
and Northern Republican men were moderately conservative but otherwise indistinguishable on national security, though recall that Southern Republicans
were a comparatively small cohort, even before being further divided by sex
(Table 4.4.D).

Shifting Preferences, Shifting Cleavages, Shifting Alignments

The postwar evolution of American politics would alter this opening summary, mottled as it already was, in a mosaic of further ways. Some of these
generalized the place of sex as a social cleavage, though not necessarily
augmenting that role. Others would make sex even more idiosyncratic within
overall partisan alignments. Thus, in the second postwar period, party as an
aligning principle would grow in importance across all four domains though in
a highly uneven fashion. Conversely, sex as an aligning principle would crash
in most domains except, ironically, in the realm where party was strongest,

namely social welfare. Finally, the impact of sexes within parties would assume a fresh overall pattern, albeit one that would prove to be only one more transient, evolutionary stage.

The modern world would then rework all this through three central developments: an increasing convergence of policy alignments, an augmented role for party attachment within these increasingly common alignments, and a bounce-back for sex as an organizing principle inside evolving parties. The result would not be a set of alignments that were uniform by party, sex, and policy preference. But it would become possible to see the interactions of the three major modern developments—overall convergence, partisan polarization, and sexual resurgence—in a way that both shaped and distinguished the modern incarnation of individual policy domains. An evolution this convoluted in its specifics—and changing specifics, at that—needs to be summarized at a relatively high level, but supportive tables still provide the associated comprehensive details.

The headline story for the aligning power of party attachment in the second postwar period was contributed by national security, previously the domain least tied to party (Table 4.5.D). National security came into the partisan alignment that had characterized social welfare in the opening period and that was emerging clearly for civil rights in this second era. If its level of polarization still trailed the level in both of those other domains, partisan polarization was actually growing most rapidly for national security, especially since, by hindsight, there was a major development in the security realm that is available to explain its change.

In this, an old basis for organizing policy conflicts, pitting isolationists against internationalists,[12] was giving way to a new basis, rooted in pursuit of the Cold War and pitting preferences for a strong defense against preferences for diplomatic engagement. By the second postwar period, the previous conflation of these two principles was effectively gone: a Cold War focus had emerged as the essence of foreign policy. Not all that long after, with the coming of the Vietnam War, an earlier national consensus on combating

Table 4.5 **Policy Preferences by Party**

	A. Social Welfare		B. Civil Rights		C. Cultural Values		D. National Security	
	Dems	*Reps*	*Dems*	*Reps*	*Dems*	*Reps*	*Dems*	*Reps*
Era 3	−.24	+.35	−.24	+.35	−.16	+.22	−.21	+.30
Era 2	−.23	+.25	−.18	+.19	−.06	+.07	−.12	+.13
Era 1	.16	+.24	−.08	+.12	−.03	+.04	−.01	+.02

Table 4.6 **Policy Preferences by Sex**

	A. Social Welfare		B. Civil Rights		C. Cultural Values		D. National Security	
	Women	*Men*	*Women*	*Men*	*Women*	*Men*	*Women*	*Men*
Era 3	−06	+.10	−.01	+.04	−.06	+.07	−.08	+.11
Era 2	−.07	+.07	+.00	−.00	−.00	+.00	−.01	+.00
Era 1	−.03	+.04	−.03	+.04	+.03	−.04	−.03	+.04

international communism disappeared as well, reinforcing this newly partisan alignment as it did so.[13]

Yet if there was a gathering momentum for policy alignment by party attachment, sex would tell the opposite story (Table 4.6). By comparison to a previously modest but generalized organizing power, sex lost most of its apparent influence in the second postwar period, only to rebound substantially in the modern world. In the opening postwar years, sex had contributed about the same level of impact to policy alignments across all four domains, which meant that it was at its comparative minimum for social welfare and its comparative maximum for national security, where sex actually outperformed party as an aligning influence. In its time, this dovetailed neatly with an argument that national security was the domain that *ought* to generate maximum impact from sex as a social cleavage.

This pattern, those alignments, and that argument proved, however, to be harbingers of absolutely nothing. In the second postwar era, sex disappeared— fell to zero—in three of the big four policy domains, one of which was national security. This made it very hard to continue contending that serious differences between men and women were intrinsic to the domain. And this time, the lone exception, the domain where the aligning power of sex rose, was social welfare. As with security in the opening years and with welfare in this second era, there were analysts who jumped in to argue that social welfare was where sex should be expected to have its maximum impact, by way of the differing economic lives of women versus men.[14]

This generalization too would be short-lived. In the modern world, the biggest gain in the aligning power of sex would return to national security, with what was once again the strongest relationship between policy preferences and the key social cleavage. In this modern era, social welfare did not regress, but it was surpassed not just by national security but also by cultural values, with an impact that was additionally striking. In the immediate postwar period, men had been the cultural liberals and women the cultural conservatives. But when sex returned as an aligning principle in the modern world, this ideological continuum was reversed, with women the liberals and men the conservatives.

THE SOCIAL ROOTS OF AMERICAN POLITICS

Table 4.7 **Policy Preferences by Sexes within Parties**

	A. Social Welfare				B. Civil Rights			
	Dem Women	Dem Men	Rep Women	Rep Men	Dem Women	Dem Men	Rep Women	Rep Men
Era 3	−.26	−.21	+.27	+.43	−.24	−.23	+.37	+.34
Era 2	−.28	−.16	+.20	+.32	−.18	−.18	+.22	+.16
Era 1	−.18	−.15	+.19	+.30	−.12	−.03	+.09	+.15
	C. Cultural Values				D. National Security			
	Dem Women	Dem Men	Rep Women	Rep Men	Dem Women	Dem Men	Rep Women	Rep Men
Era 3	−.20	−.11	+.16	+.26	−.28	−.12	+.25	+.34
Era 2	−.06	−.05	+.06	+.07	−.12	−.12	+.13	+.14
Era 1	+.01	−.10	+.05	+.02	−.06	+.02	−.01	+.05

Table 4.7 gathers the story of policy preferences by sexes within parties, now for four major domains in all three temporal periods. The volatility of policy relationships to sex, and thus the instability of sex within partisan alignments, argues against a detailed tour of everything inside this table. Numerous individual idiosyncrasies remain available to the curious, but the overall result does not lend itself to simple summaries, very unlike the counterpart tables for class, race, and religion. Rather, the larger implications of Table 4.7 center on the change engine associated with the evolving role of sex as a social cleavage, involving a changing overall party balance whose mechanics will be elaborated in the final substantive section of this chapter.

Across all three postwar periods, party attachment trumped sex as an aligning principle for social welfare, with Democrats left of Republicans in every sexualized party in every period (Table 4.7.A), though across all three, sex served as a secondary aligning principle inside party attachment, with women left of men in both parties. So Democrats were not only left of Republicans but also left of the national average, Republicans were not only right of Democrats but also right of the national average, and women were left of men (and men right of women) within each of those parties.

Knowing this welfare alignment and its evolutionary path, it is possible to see that civil rights in the opening postwar period offered a weaker version of the same pattern: Democrats on the left, Republicans on the right, and women left of men inside both parties (Table 4.7.B). A dominant role for party attachment on civil rights would be indisputably confirmed in the successor era, as the two parties polarized in their rights preferences. Yet at the same time, sex lost its modest aligning power in the rights domain, and while a policy alignment by party would increase even more strongly in the modern era, sex would stand out for the opposite reason, failing to regain any aligning power in the rights domain for the modern world.

Cultural values was distinguished in the immediate postwar years by the absence of aligning influences from either party or sex, apart from the idiosyncratic liberalism of Democratic men (Table 4.7.C). In the successor period, party attachment began to show a modest organizing power, with moderately liberal Democrats facing moderately conservative Republicans, but sex remained absent as an organizing influence. Only in the modern world did party attachment confirm its place as an indisputable organizer for cultural preferences, accompanied this time by an evident secondary organizing power for sex, with women left of men inside each of the increasingly polarized parties.

Originally the great dissident domain, in that sex had a larger aligning influence than party, national security saw the rise of a clear partisan polarization of its own in the second postwar era, coupled with a collapse of any organizing power for sex. Democrats were on the left, Republicans were on the right, and both men and women were indistinguishable within those parties. The power of party attachment was then strongly augmented in the modern world, nearly catching up with both social welfare and civil rights, while sex experienced the same rebound as it did with cultural values, giving national security another nested alignment by sexes within parties.

For the nation as a whole, the big change in the role of party attachment as a shaping influence on policy alignments came with national security in the second postwar period and with cultural values in the modern era. For the nation as a whole, the big change in the contribution of sex to these evolving partisan alignments was a general decline in the second postwar period, sparing only social welfare, followed by a general recovery in the modern world, leaving only civil rights without much further influence on policy alignments from sex. In the nation as a whole, finally, the four policy domains retained some distinguishing characteristics, though these could be well described—and implicitly connected—by the interaction of policy preference, social cleavage, party attachment, and, last but only sometimes least, geographic region.

So far, this section has ignored the prospect that region was a driving force behind policy convergence, partisan polarization, and sexual resurgence; or that region was just a correlate of their joint evolution; or that region was at least a clear brake on this evolution, delaying though not ultimately derailing it. The need to interpret strengthening partisan alignments by turning quickly to—and then integrating—regional distinctions would inevitably become less pressing as they usurped at least some of what were previously regional influences. Yet the reintroduction of region remains essential to untangling the various contributors to

Table 4.8 Policy Preferences by Sexes within Parties: The Regions

	A. Social Welfare				B. Civil Rights			
	Dem Women	*Dem Men*	*Rep Women*	*Rep Men*	*Dem Women*	*Dem Men*	*Rep Women*	*Rep Men*
Era 3	−.26	−.21	+.27	+.43	−.24	−.23	+.37	+.34
South	−.28	−.24	+.28	+.42	−.26	−.34	+.38	+.36
North	−.26	−.19	+.26	+.43	−.24	−.17	+.36	+.32
Era 2	−.28	−.16	+.20	+.32	−.18	−.18	+.22	+.16
South	−.31	−.17	+.22	+.37	−.12	−.10	+.29	+.28
North	−.27	−.15	+.20	+.30	−.21	−.22	+.20	+.14
Era 1	−.18	−.15	+.19	+.30	−.12	−.03	+.09	+.15
South	−.01	−.06	+.20	+.32	+.15	+.18	+.32	+.09
North	−.24	−.17	+.17	+.32	−.26	−.11	+.06	+.13

	C. Cultural Values				D. National Security			
	Dem Women	*Dem Men*	*Rep Women*	*Rep Men*	*Dem Women*	*Dem Men*	*Rep Women*	*Rep Men*
Era 3	−.20	−.11	+.18	+.26	−.28	−.10	+.25	+.36
South	−.10	−.01	+.25	+.21	−.18	−.02	+.29	+.44
North	−.27	−.16	+.13	+.28	−.35	−.15	+.22	+.32
Era 2	−.05	−.06	+.07	+.06	−.12	−.12	+.13	+.14
South	+.06	+.08	+.17	+.12	−.01	+.03	+.21	+.21
North	−.14	−.13	+.04	+.04	−.19	−.21	+.10	+.11
Era 1	+.01	−.10	+.05	+.02	−.06	+.04	−.01	+.05
South	+.11	+.01	+.19	+.13	+.02	+.04	+.01	+.05
North	−.01	−.11	+.04	−.00	−.10	+.03	−.01	+.05

partisan alignment across time, and to placing sex as a social cleavage within that tangle, so Table 4.8 brings back the story of policy, sex, and party in four major domains, now stratified by geographic region.

Social welfare began the postwar period with all three organizing principles in evidence—party, sex, and region—but with party dominant, region a powerful secondary influence, and sex possessing further systematic influence only in the North (Table 4.8.A). The big news in the successor period was that the South had come fully into sync with the national alignment. Yet the dynamic accompanying that change—party up and region down—featured an augmented role for sex as well, in both parties and in both regions.[15] For the modern period, those effects would be confirmed through alignments that retained the power of party, retained the secondary influence of sex, but marginalized region more or less entirely.

Civil rights began the postwar period with all three organizing principles in evidence, but with region clearly dominant, party an obvious but secondary influence, and sex playing a tertiary role only in the North (Table 4.8.B). The big news in the successor period was that the South adopted a policy alignment parallel to that of the nation as a whole, though region retained enough influence to hold all Southern cohorts clearly right of their Northern counterparts, while sex disappeared as even a tertiary influence, for the North and not just the South. The modern world then essentially completed the convergence of the rights and the welfare domains, leaving a regional influence on civil rights only among Democratic men while showing no systematic influence by sex.

Cultural values opened the postwar era showing a strong policy alignment by geographic region, with only hints of any potential influence for party or sex, apart from the greater liberalism of Democratic men (Table 4.8.C). Region retained its dominant organizing place in the successor period, though the two Democratic cohorts were now left of the two Republican cohorts in both regions, while sex was now absent as an aligning influence in either region. So it would be the modern era before party attachment became the dominant influence on policy alignments for cultural values, though inside this newly partisan structure, region retained its greatest influence among the four policy domains, while sex broke through systematically for the first time, with women left of men in all four sexualized parties.

That left national security, the one domain that had privileged sex over both party and region in the opening postwar period, when women were left of men in both parties and both regions (Table 4.10.D). Yet these effects were small, so when both party and region surged as aligning influences in the successor era, their ability to banish sex was not really surprising. Party attachment would then expand its organizing power in the modern world, with Democrats liberal and Republicans conservative. Region would sustain a clear secondary power, with the North more liberal and the South more conservative for all four sexualized parties. But sex would be resuscitated, with women clearly left of men and men clearly right of women in both parties and both regions.

Sex and a Changing Party Balance

That is a collective picture of evolutionary trajectories for four major policy domains. Its macro-story concerns the rise of party attachment as an organizing principle and the decline of geographic region as its leading competitor. But woven through this core narrative is another complex and convoluted story, of sex as a social cleavage. By comparison to the other major cleavages, sex proves to be less consistent and more labile. As a principle of policy organization in its own right, it rises, falls, and rises again. Even then, it does so in divergent ways in different policy domains. Despite all that, these variable aligning differences for men versus women were capable of playing important roles in specific policy domains at particular points in time, remaining consequential into the modern era in three of the four major domains.

Yet over and above this winding path through four individual realms—and this must be the larger point for any conclusion about the impact of sex as a social cleavage—differences between men and women were also clearly tied to changes in *party balance* for the nation as a whole. Indeed, this shifting balance constituted nothing less than another fundamental engine of change in American politics, an engine with increasing consequences as party attachment rose as an aligning influence. Between the immediate postwar years and the modern era, men and women actually changed their aggregate partisan loyalties. Democrats began as more male and became more female; Republicans began as more female and became more male. Yet the trade-off, while reciprocal, was not equal. Men moved more than women, so Republicans gained more than Democrats.[16] And along the way, the resulting shift in the balance of party identifiers made an autonomous contribution to the impact of sex on partisan alignments.

What was driving this particular—and almost definitionally consequential—change? For partisan alignments by social class, change had been driven by the structural instantiation of class interests, and then by shifts in the social situations from which these interests sprang and to which they responded. For alignments by racial background, change was instead grounded in the formal process of voter enfranchisement, yielding major shifts in the social composition of the electorate itself, followed by ongoing mutual adjustments. And for alignments by religious denomination, change was driven by yet a third major engine, namely partisan mobilization, involving the discovery of implicit policy preferences that could be consciously activated by the political parties in response to evolving shifts in the larger society.

None of these three means of restructuring partisan alignments were an obvious fit to sex as a social cleavage. Immediate postwar alignments by sex were not instantiated at all; they continued to shift, both individually and collectively. There was no formal enfranchisement benefiting one sex or the other; the enfranchisement of women was a huge example of just such a change, but it had occurred a half-century earlier. And no one uncovered some deep latent preference that became a continuing key to the behavior of men or women, much less of the two jointly. Instead, this particular change has to be tracked

Men, Women, and Policy Preferences   103

backward, beginning with the changing balance of party attachments between women and men and moving back to the links between sex and policy preference that served as *incentives* for a change in party attachment and a resulting alteration in party balance.

In the immediate postwar years, self-identified membership in the two national parties did not show much difference by sex. Both in fact featured female majorities (Table 4.9.A). Inside this common majority, Democrats were slightly more male and Republicans slightly more female, but the difference—three percentage points—was not impressive. Yet by the modern era, the two parties were not only increasingly disparate by sex but also actually fronted opposite majorities, the Democrats solidly female and the Republicans narrowly male. On the way to this resolution, the share of Democratic identifiers who were female increased substantially, as did the share of Republican identifiers who were male.[17] This is the development that fueled substantial subsequent attention to what became known as a gender *gap*.

This gap can be further stratified through its structural underpinnings, dividing the sexual difference in party identifications into party activists versus their rank and file (Table 4.9.B). Absent the activists, the two rank and files in the immediate postwar years were a trifle less distinguishable by sex, though both

Table 4.9 **Sexes within Parties across the Postwar Years**

A. Party Attachment by Sex

		Men	Women
Era 1, 1952–1968	Dems	48%	52%
	Reps	45%	55%
Era 3, 1992–2008	Dems	40%	60%
	Reps	51%	49%

B. Partisan Population by Sex

		Men	Women
Era 1, 1952–1968	DAcs	54%	46%
	DRFs	47%	53%
	RRFs	45%	55%
	RAcs	46%	54%
Era 3, 1992–2008	DAcs	48%	52%
	DRFs	38%	62%
	RRFs	49%	51%
	RAcs	56%	44%

still showed female majorities and the Democrats were still the more male of the two. Yet stratified this way, the two sets of party activists looked notably different. Both active parties were more male than their rank and files, but this difference was trivial among Republicans, who remained majority female among their activists too. Yet the Democrats fronted an actual male majority in their active party. So if this activist difference by sex was not as impressive as some counterpart differences by class, race, or religion, it was not insubstantial, with Republican activists more closely reflecting not just their own rank and file by sex but also the Democratic rank and file.

Still, the more important point is that by the modern era, everything had changed. Both rank and files did remain majority female, albeit solidly so among Democrats and only marginally so among Republicans. Yet what had been a gender gap of two percentage points between the two rank and files in the early years, with the Republicans more female, had become a contrary gap of eleven percentage points in the modern world, with the Democrats more female this time. And the same general reversal was even stronger among party activists.[18] Where the Democrats had been male-led in the opening years, fifty-four to forty-six men over women, they were now female-led, fifty-two to forty-eight women over men. Conversely, where the Republicans had been female-led in that opening period, fifty-four to forty-six women over men, they were now solidly male-led, fifty-six to forty-four men over women.[19]

That is an evolutionary story for the gender gap as originally defined, and for an exposition of the relationship between sex and party attachment, it is sufficient. Yet for purposes of studying the dynamics of partisan *change*, and especially for locating the policy incentives that drove it, this approach is misleading in two senses, one empirical and one methodological. The lesser of these involves what we have come to understand as the practical empirics of party structure. Empirical research on party activists, the individuals who do the operational work of the political parties and whose policy preferences are differentially important as a result, has long found that they are far less likely to switch party attachments than their rank and files, a reticence that has only increased as one gets closer to the modern era.[20] This finding suggests that a hunt for party switchers is likely to be obscured by including activists in the enterprise, and that the hunt for a change in party balance should be focused on the party rank and files.

The larger of two misleading approaches to a changing party balance and the policy incentives that support it is methodological, involving the direction in which the appropriate data are percentaged. An approach focused on sex and partisan change rather than a gender gap for its own sake must percentage the sexes by party rather than the parties by sex. Doing this yields immediate dividends by telling a different story, one much more directly related to changes

Men, Women, and Policy Preferences 105

Table 4.10 **Parties within Sexes across the Postwar Years: Sex by Partisan Population**

		DRFs	*RRFs*
Era 1, 1952–1968	Men	62%	38%
	Women	60%	40%
Era 3, 1992–2008	Men	51%	49%
	Women	62%	38%

in party balance. Table 4.10 percentages the data from Table 4.9.B in this opposite direction: not men and women as a share of each party, but Democrats and Republicans as a share of each sex. That allows partisan change by sex to drive the analysis, comparing the place of party attachment within sexes, looking at the comparative scope of increases and decreases for each party, and informing a judgment about the comparative size of the two effects.[21]

In some ways, a picture of sexes by party does not look terribly different from the previous picture of parties within sexes. Female majorities still show up for both Democrats and Republicans, while the Democrats still look ever so modestly more male in the early years by comparison to the Republicans. Yet the critical picture for the modern era, the one focusing more directly on changes in party balance, now looks strikingly different. Rank-and-file women do move up as a share of the Democratic Party, from 60% to 62%. But rank-and-file men move up much more as a share of the Republican Party, from 40% to 49%. As a change engine, then, party balance, as opposed to sexual balance, offers a net increment to the Republican Party. By extension, the power of partisan distinction by sex has increased overall, but a much larger part of this increase belongs to the Republicans and not to the Democrats.

If this were extrapolated directly to electoral politics, with Republicans possessing an extra eleven percentage points among men in the first postwar era while the Democrats had possessed an extra two points among women, then Thomas E. Dewey would have been president in 1948, defeating Harry Truman, and Richard M. Nixon would have gotten there in his first try in 1960, defeating John Kennedy rather than having to wait for a retest in 1968. By the same token, had the Democrats not shed 11% of their male support while gaining that further 2% among women in the modern era, Al Gore would have been president in 2000, defeating George W. Bush without the need for a court challenge; John Kerry would have unhorsed Bush in 2004, had the latter somehow survived the 2000 contest; and Hillary Clinton would have become president in 2016, acquiring a majority in the Electoral College and not just a plurality in the popular vote.

This leads to the inevitable closing questions: What was it that drove a noteworthy share of previously Democratic men to switch to the Republican Party? Conversely, what was it that caused another, lesser, but still substantial share of previously Republican women to cross over to the Democrats? And more specifically in both cases, what was it about their individual preferences that led to a powerful collective shift in party balance? Alas, our data—or any of which we know—do not allow the isolation of the two key populations of party switchers on a scale sufficiently large and temporally extended to be reliable. On the other hand, there is a silver lining.

An analysis of partisan alignments across time, stratified by sex, does make it possible to highlight the policy domains where the sexualized party cohorts—Democratic women, Democratic men, Republican women, and Republican men—were farthest out of line with, and in that sense most alienated from, the policy preferences of their active parties. Specifically, Table 4.11 asks which of the four cohorts among the rank and file faced the greatest disjunctions between their own preferences and the position of their active parties, and hence the largest institutionalized incentives to "correct" these misalignments.

We know the collective preferences of party activists. We know the individual preferences of members of the party rank and file. So it is not difficult to give each rank-and-file respondent a score for the distance between their own policy preferences and the collective position of the two active parties. These *representational gaps*, the distance between their own policy preferences and the collective preference of the two active parties, to the right of those preferences among Democrats and to the left of those preferences among Republicans, became the leading structural incentives for party switches, and thus the institutionalized seedbeds for what became a noteworthy partisan reversal.

Table 4.11 **Representational Gap by Sex across the Postwar Period**

		DW	DM	RW	RM
Era 1	Social Welfare	+.02	+.04	<u>−.25</u>	+.12
	Civil Rights	+.06	+.13	−.06	−.12
	Cultural Values	+.06	−.04	+.09	+.01
	National Security	+.01	+.08	−.01	+.07
Era 3	Social Welfare	+.05	+.10	<u>−.29</u>	−.12
	Civil Rights	+.16	<u>+.21</u>	−.09	−.12
	Cultural Values	+.15	<u>+.25</u>	−.12	−.03
	National Security	+.10	<u>+.28</u>	−.05	−.15

Programmatic disjunctions greater than .20 are underlined.

Men, Women, and Policy Preferences

In the first postwar period, rank-and-file Republican women were the cohort with the greatest misalignment between their policy preferences and the programmatic positions taken by activists in their chosen party, an alienation that was crystallized in the domain of social welfare in the period when welfare issues were indisputably at the center of American politics. Perhaps more surprisingly, these women remained the Republican cohort most out of line with their party in the modern world, still via social welfare forty years later. So while net gains across time favored men and Republicans, there was a significant cohort of women who moved toward the Democrats. And among them, the segment with the greatest incentive for doing so was the rank-and-file Republican women who were misaligned on social welfare.

By comparison, neither sexual cohort within the Democratic rank and file, female or male, had a serious problem with the policy positions of their active party in the early postwar years. The largest representational gap surfaced among Democratic men on civil rights, but this was modest compared to the problems of Republican women on social welfare and unimpressive compared to the problems that these Democratic men would face in the modern world. Indeed, what jumps out of the table in this modern world is the veritable cascade of policy problems for rank-and-file Democratic men. Now, substantive differences with their putative leadership are nearly everywhere, among men who are obviously and disproportionately encouraged to move toward the Republicans on national security as well as civil rights and cultural values.

In the end, Republican women who were stressed by considerations of public policy on social welfare remained the party identifiers most distant from the active Republican Party.[22] This made them the Republicans with the strongest policy grounds for moving to the Democrats, and thus the ones with the strongest incentives to constitute the female increase among Democratic identifiers. Yet Democratic men engaged by anything *other than* social welfare became the party identifiers most distant from the active Democratic Party. In turn, this made them the Democrats with the strongest—and multiple—policy grounds for moving to the Republicans, and thus the ones with the strongest incentives to constitute the male increase among Republican identifiers. And they did in fact move more than four times as much proportionately as the female shift in the other direction.

Policy Preferences, Sex, and a Changing Party Balance

Sex, fourth of what are usually treated as the four major social cleavages in American society, was the one with the most checkered relationship to policy preferences, varying the most across the four major domains as well as within them across time. Sex began with a mild but essentially equivalent relationship to all four, women to the left and men to the right, with the exception of cultural values, where this ideological direction was reversed. Weak but equivalent policy relationships did mean that the comparative importance of sex as an organizing principle for partisan alignments depended on the nature of the two other principal relationships to policy preferences, namely party attachment or geographic region.

In this regard, sex was clearly outweighed by party attachment on social welfare, although a modest alignment by sex inside a much stronger alignment by party would be the one such relationship that proved stable across time. Sex was instead outweighed by geographic region on both civil rights and cultural values. A tertiary relationship to sex for civil rights did survive inside party attachment in the North but not in the South, while both party and sex were simply jumbled in their impact on cultural values. The one domain where sex surpassed both party and region, though the triumph was modest, was national security, also the one domain where sex was thought to have the most obvious policy relationship, with women expected to be dovish (liberal) and men hawkish (conservative). Initial policy alignments in early postwar surveys did not disappoint.

As a social cleavage, sex again showed a nearly equivalent relationship to the main policy domains in the successor era, but this time for an ironic reason. Sex did continue its original relationship to preferences on social welfare, with women to the left and men to their right inside both parties. But this time, the three other domains showed nearly equivalent relationships to sex because this relationship fell to zero in all three. Women and men were not more liberal or more conservative on civil rights, cultural values, or even national security. Party rose and region fell as aligning influences for civil rights, but sex fell too. Party rose and region was sustained on cultural values, but sex fell again. And party rose but so did region on national security, as sex fell once more, killing the theory that it was intrinsically connected to security preferences.

In the modern era, sex continued to demonstrate a propensity to change policy alignments from period to period within domains, while adding variety to its impacts across them. Social welfare remained the exception, as party and sex continued to expand a basic relationship instantiated in the immediate postwar period. Yet sex rebounded as an organizing influence for both cultural values and national security, while party expanded in both domains and region was sustained inside augmented alignments by party. That made civil rights the lone domain where party rose, region fell, but sex did not enjoy a resurgence.

Overall, then, sex ran far behind social class, racial background, or religious denomination when measured by the temporal stability of its relationships and the propensity for policy links to expand in anything approximating a linear manner. This did not mean that specific incarnations of a policy relationship to sex, for example with national security in the opening period or with cultural values in the modern era, were not consequential in their own right at a specified time. Yet the analytic risk in focusing on constantly changing patterns of alignment was that this variety plus its labile character would suggest that there was no systematic contribution to partisan alignments from sex as a social cleavage.

That would have been entirely wrong, for in fact, *party balance* in American society, a crucial underpinning to all those partisan alignments, was implicitly, subtly, but substantially driven by differences between the sexes. Differences by sex in the composition of the parties—a gender gap—did become a subject for elite discussion and even data collection during the second of our three postwar periods, ironically the period when policy differences by sex declined to zero in most major domains. Yet a long-term shift in the contribution of sex to aggregate party balances was under way and would reach impressive levels in the modern era. This shift would contribute the fourth and final major engine of change to a picture of the evolution of partisan alignments in postwar politics.

Seen this way, via the partisan divide among sexes rather than the sexual divide within parties, there were to be gains on both sides of the sexual aisle. The share of women who were self-described Democrats increased, as did the share of men who were self-described Republicans. That was a reasonable summary of statistical difference in party attachment by sex. But stratified the other way around, through partisan balance within the sexes, Republican gains among men proved considerably larger than Democratic gains among women for the postwar period as a whole. Moreover, this direct impact from sex as a social cleavage, far more than the wandering mediated paths by way of policy relationships, had consequences everywhere, most especially by providing a different numerical base for partisan alignments in all four major domains.

How could this be so, for a social cleavage with such a meandering connection to policy preferences? Largely because the two sexes were ordinarily responsive to entirely different policy stimuli—which is to say: in order to have a substantial impact on party balance, men and women did not need to respond to the same policy incentives as a route to party switching, much less respond in a reflexively opposite direction. They could lean in one ideological direction for women and the other ideological direction for men in any given domain, yet have one sex but not the other moved to reconsider the party attachments associated with policy preferences in that domain. This meant that men and women could move—even to the point of changing parties—in response to very different policy domains.

And indeed they did. Thus, women who switched parties were disproportionately likely to move from Republican to Democratic, and women who made this party switch were disproportionately likely to be out of sync with the active Republican Party on social welfare. Conversely, men who switched parties were disproportionately likely to move from Democratic to Republican, yet men who made this move were disproportionately likely to be out of sync with Democratic Party activists on nearly everything except social welfare, beginning with national security but including civil rights and cultural values.

So it was this combination of misalignments by sex in specific policy domains that would shift the collective balance of party identifications in American society, generating a substantial and wide-ranging impact on partisan alignments even as it was not (and did not need to be) accompanied by policy changes specific to both sexes simultaneously. In that way, the changing balance between the two parties became the fourth great engine of change in postwar politics, joining the instantiation of interests, the reform of voter enfranchisement, and the partisan mobilization of latent interests. In the process, sex was confirmed as the fourth social cleavage with major impacts on that politics, joining social class, racial background, and religious denomination.

Conclusion

The Social Evolution of Postwar Politics

Partisan Alignments since the Second World War

How do public wishes become policy conflicts in American politics? And what drives change in the politics of those conflicts across time? The search for an answer has returned, over and over, to the notion of *partisan alignment*. Policy conflicts are rooted in the major cleavages that characterize American society, most especially social class, racial background, religious denomination, and sex. Yet explicit conflicts over the policy preferences associated with these cleavages evolve largely through their linkage to political parties, with the result that tracing this linkage, both its initial forging and its subsequent progression, is the central analytic tool not just for following political change but also for seeking out the differing engines that drive it.

Over time, partisan alignments became central to all four of the major domains for postwar policy conflict—social welfare, civil rights, national security, and cultural values—albeit arriving at different times and progressing in different manners. Yet there were other available means to link public preferences to policymaking, where the strongest alternative was geographic region, fostering regional rather than partisan policy alignments. So the tension between party and region had to be a major focus of the overall evolution of this postwar politics. One did not reliably drive the other—it was not just regions up and parties down or vice versa—but partisanship would continue to rise as a structuring influence for public preferences, while region would continue to decline, though not disappear, even in an increasingly nationalized politics.

The Social Roots of American Politics. Regina L. Wagner and Byron E. Shafer, Oxford University Press.
© Oxford University Press 2022. DOI: 10.1093/oso/9780197650844.003.0006

That said, too many analyses of the ostensible roots of political conflict begin and end with policy preferences and party attachment. This misses the initial—and fundamental—structuring influences involving the major cleavages in American society, reliable seedbeds for preference divisions. More or less inherently, these cleavages shaped personal experiences and conveyed political interests:

- One, social class, was a substantial influence on policy preferences from the start, expanding modestly but relentlessly thereafter.
- Another, racial background, would explode in the early postwar years, with policy divisions that were deeper but more narrow than those emanating from social class.
- A third, religious denomination, was largely dormant in the early years, rising to political prominence as time passed and as active partisans came to see a religious potential for organizing politics.
- And the fourth, sex, would have the most mottled relationship to policy preferences but the most direct connection to party attachment.

So the task of a concluding chapter becomes straightforward. It must assemble a composite picture of partisan alignments and their evolution, including the final links in an evolutionary chain that runs from social cleavages to policy preferences to party attachments to institutionalized political conflict. To that end, this chapter begins with an analysis of the overarching partisan convergence that emerged across all four policy domains. It moves to the contrasting decline of regional alignments as the main alternative to party attachment. It doubles back to the evolving place of major social cleavages, first in their own right and then for their place within that overarching convergence, which sets up a concise but comprehensive closing summary of the social evolution of postwar American politics.

Partisan Convergence across Policy Domains

Public preferences were indisputably aligned by party attachment in only one major domain when the first survey for what became the American National Election Study (ANES) went into the field for the 1952 presidential election. That domain was social welfare, the central policy concern injected into American politics by the New Deal. By 1952, it came effectively prepackaged with a partisan alignment.[1] Democrats were more likely to be liberal and Republicans conservative on welfare policy, and, said the other way around, welfare liberals were more likely to be Democrats and welfare conservatives to be Republicans (Table C.1.A). Moreover, this relationship would not be transient. Partisan differences on welfare preferences would increase in the second postwar era and increase again in the third. In the process, social welfare would provide not only the policy spine for postwar political conflict but also the analytic template for comparing partisan alignments across policy domains.

Civil rights would be confirmed as the rising realm for policy conflict by the second of these postwar eras. Yet it was only gathering steam in 1952, with a weak echo of the alignment that already characterized social welfare[2] (Table C.1.B). Indeed, politics in the previous generation, the one reaching from the high New Deal into the postwar world, suggested that civil rights was unlikely to follow in the footsteps of social welfare. The policy coalitions necessary to pass the New Deal had required the support of economic liberals who were racial conservatives, and Franklin Roosevelt never lost sight of that fact. Yet in the second postwar era, public preferences on civil rights were to assume the same general alignment as those on social welfare, liberals and Democrats to the left versus conservatives and Republicans to the right, a result that would grow only stronger in the third era, to the point of full partisan equality between the two domains.

By contrast, national security, despite the "hottest" part of the Cold War in these early years and despite American leadership in this international conflict, showed effectively no relationship to party attachment (Table C.1.C). Hawks and doves were as likely to be Democrats as Republicans, with Democrats and Republicans as likely to be hawks as doves.[3] Yet partisan neutrality would give way to partisan alignment in the successor period, as the Cold War acquired a party-related edge, most centrally via the war in Vietnam, with Democrats dovish and Republicans hawkish. If the result still lagged the counterpart alignment for civil rights, it was already stronger than that alignment had been when it had emerged incipiently in the preceding era. So national security was evidently on the partisan rise, and it would move close to parity with both civil rights and social welfare in the third postwar era.

Like national security, cultural values, the last of the big four policy domains, was close to unaligned by party attachment in the years immediately following

Table C.1 **Partisan Alignments across Time: The Comparative Evolution**

	A. Social Welfare		B. Civil Rights		C. National Security		D. Cultural Values	
	Dems	*Reps*	*Dems*	*Reps*	*Dems*	*Reps*	*Dems*	*Reps*
Era 3	−.24	+.36	−.24	+.36	−.20	+.30	−.16	+.22
Era 2	−.24	+.26	−.16	+.19	−.12	+.13	−.06	+.07
Era 1	−.17	+.24	−.08	+.12	−.01	+.02	−.03	+.04

World War II. Yet the roots of this partisan neutrality were otherwise very different.[4] What were the hottest years of the Cold War in the domain of national security were instead years of apparent dormancy for cultural issues and cultural conflict (Table C.1.D). Central to politics in earlier periods, conflicts over the values governing social life appeared to have lost their substantive potency as well as their partisan bite. Yet where national security would acquire just such a bite in the successor period, cultural values would remain largely unstructured by partisanship—until an indisputably partisan alignment finally surfaced in the modern era, bringing a cultural policy alignment into conformity with the other major domains while completing a structural convergence across all four.

So a previously disparate American politics, with divergent partisan alignments, had apparently assumed a common organizational character in the modern world, for policy domains that were (and still are) hugely different in their substantive content. All four began the postwar period with policy alignments that were individually distinctive in their connection to party attachment. Table C.1 isolated their evolution by comparing ideological scores for Democrats and Republicans in four major domains for three postwar periods. Table C.2 uses those figures to produce summary measures for the *distance between* a partisan alignment on social welfare, the template for policy conflict in the immediate postwar years, and the partisan alignments characterizing each of the other domains.

To that end, the entries for Table C.2 compare (1) the partisan gap between Democrats for the two domains in question, (2) the partisan gap between Republicans for the same two domains, and (3) the sum of those partisan gaps for the two parties together. For example, on the way to the most complete instance of partisan convergence, the gap between Democrats on social welfare and civil rights in the opening period was .08, the gap between Republicans for the same period was .12, and the total gap was thus .20[5] (Table C.2.A). Yet by the modern world, all three gaps had shrunk effectively to zero. So what was originally a clear-cut difference between the strength of two partisan alignments, favoring social welfare over civil rights, was now essentially an identity, with the two domains more or less indistinguishable.

Table C.2 **Partisan Convergence across Domains: The Coming of Unidimensional Politics**

| | A. SW and CR | | | B. SW and NS | | | C. SW and CV | | |
	Dem	Reps	Total	Dems	Reps	Total	Dems	Reps	Total
Era 3	.00	.00	.00	.04	.06	.10	.08	.14	.22
Era 2	.08	.07	.15	.13	.13	.26	.18	.19	.37
Era 1	.09	.12	.21	.16	.22	.38	.14	.20	.34

The difference in partisan alignments between social welfare and national security was far greater in the opening period, almost double the distance between social welfare and civil rights. On the one hand, this divergence was declining among Democrats, among Republicans, and among the two together in the successor period, incipiently moving toward partisan convergence (Table C.2.B). On the other hand, the remaining differences were larger in the second postwar era than they had been for the original gap between social welfare and civil rights. This made the convergence between social welfare and national security in the modern world all the more striking, since this gap too converged sharply, not just toward social welfare but in effect toward civil rights as well.

That left cultural values with the most stubborn resistance to convergence. In the opening postwar period, the policy alignment on cultural values was every bit as distant as national security from the counterpart alignment on social welfare (Table C.2.C). And while civil rights left room for the prospect that it might yet produce an alignment similar to social welfare, neither national security nor cultural values offered any comparable promise. Moreover, and unlike national security, cultural values did not move toward social welfare in the successor era. The two-party gap between the two domains was no closer in this second period, and if Republicans converged a little, Democrats actually moved a trifle farther away. Yet the drive toward a common alignment would characterize the modern world even here. If cultural values was still farthest of the three other domains from a diagnostic welfare alignment, it was nevertheless moving toward that alignment among Democrats, Republicans, and of course the two together.

Yet if the policy disputes central to American politics since the Second World War were converging in their overall alignment—collapsing toward a single organizing dimension—this evolution became all the more impressive because it was accompanied by a second shared development, one that made the production of a common alignment more difficult. This second development was partisan polarization, the degree to which policy realms that were connected to party attachment saw the two parties moving farther apart instead of closer together.[6] So as the three other domains were converging toward a pattern inaugurated by social welfare, the welfare domain was simultaneously moving away from its own initial position, moving the ideological goalposts in the process and increasing the change necessary for any other domain to converge with social welfare.

A simple way to track this growing mutual polarization is to focus on the ideological distance between aggregate Democrats and aggregate Republicans across the three postwar periods, 1950–1970, 1970–1990, and 1990–2010. Table C.3 extracts these distances from Table C.1. For social welfare, this produced a further 50% expansion, from a distance of .41 in Era 1 (−.17 for the Democrats to +.24 for the Republicans) to one of .60 in Era 3 (−.24 for the Democrats to +

Table C.3 **Partisan Polarization within Domains: The Onmarch of Party Attachment**

	A. Social Welfare	B. Civil Rights	C. National Security	D. Cultural Values
Era 3	.60	.60	.50	.38
Era 2	.50	.35	.25	.13
Era 1	.41	.20	.03	.07

.36 for the Republicans). As impressive as this was in absolute terms, it was actually the smallest proportionate increase of the four domains. So if ideological differences by party attachment expanded even on welfare policy, every other domain was to polarize more steeply, far more steeply in fact.

For civil rights, first to come into a common alignment with social welfare, this was a tripling between Era 1 and Era 3, from .20 to .60 (Table C.3.B). For national security, beginning with a near absence of any relationship to party attachment, it was gargantuan: from .03 in Era 1 to .50 in Era 3 (Table C.3.C). If cultural values continued to lag the other three in its level of polarization, it made by far the largest proportional increase between the second era and the modern world, tripling in one generation from .13 in Era 2 to .38 in Era 3, while generating by far the most explosive modern change as it did so. Accordingly, all four domains not only moved into increased ideological conformity (Table C.3.D) but also managed to do so while the benchmark domain, social welfare, was requiring constantly augmented change in order to allow overall convergence with it.

Partisan Convergence and Regional Decline

The great alternative to policy alignment by party attachment when the postwar period began, and indeed the great alternative throughout most of American history, was policy alignment by geographic region. In the earliest days of the republic, the key regional divide pitted the coasts against the interior. Yet well before the Civil War, this critical divide had shifted to North versus South, a division that became so entrenched that it was still in place at the end of the Second World War. The high New Deal, from 1932 to 1938, suggested that a truly national politics, independent of regional roots, might be in process. But as early as 1938, this vision had proven premature, as regional divisions of all sorts, but especially North versus South, returned to their long-standing role in structuring (and explaining) American politics.[7]

Such a history does suggest that a search for the social roots of American politics, along with the means by which these social seedbeds generate policy

Conclusion

Table C.4 **The Great Competing Principle: Geographic Region across Time**

	A. Social Welfare		B. Civil Rights		C. National Security		D. Cultural Values	
	North	*South*	*North*	*South*	*North*	*South*	*North*	*South*
Era 3	+.01	−.02	+.03	−.01	−.03	+.09	−.05	+.07
Era 2	+.01	−.04	−.02	+.04	−.05	+.08	−.04	+.09
Era 1	−.01	+.02	−.06	+.16	−.01	+.02	−.03	+.08

alignments, should begin by paying attention to both party attachment and geographic region. In order to isolate the impacts of both party and region while distinguishing between them, Table C.4 gathers policy preferences by region, North versus South, for the four major domains across three postwar periods. The result is a kind of baseline, distinguishing domains where region appeared to generate underlying differences *before* the critical intervening influence of party, while comparing them to policy domains where region contributed no such apparently inherent differences.

Seen this way, the regions were most sharply divided—the ideological space between North and South was at its greatest—on civil rights in the opening postwar period (Table C.4.B). The two regions were also clearly distinguished by public preferences on cultural values, though the domain as a whole did not figure heavily in active policy conflicts at the time (Table C.4.D). By contrast, the regions were little different when seen through public preferences on social welfare or national security, suggesting little intrinsic potential for regional influence, though social welfare was already well organized by party, while national security showed neither regional nor partisan influences (Table C.4.A and C).

This regional story was to be shuffled substantially in the successor era. Region continued to contribute little to policy alignments on social welfare, an irrelevance that would extend into the third postwar period. In line with the coming of party as the dominant aligning influence on civil rights, the regional divide was to lose more than two-thirds of its distinction in this second era, falling only farther in the modern world. Yet at the same time, cultural values and national security would displace civil rights as policy domains with the greatest ideological distance between regions, courtesy of a deep-dyed cultural conservatism and a strong military tradition in the South. Both regional differences would continue into the modern world.

That was a portrait of policy alignments by region on their own terms, that is, in the absence of competing principles for policy organization. Yet party was on the rise from the start, while region and party inevitably interacted from the earliest postwar years. So Table C.5 displays policy preferences by party attachment and geographic region simultaneously, that is, parties within regions and regions

118   THE SOCIAL ROOTS OF AMERICAN POLITICS

within parties. Carved this way, the story of social welfare remained straightforward. Not only were welfare preferences the lead register for policy alignments by party from the start, but also region competed at all only among Southern Democrats, and then only in this first period, in a difference that was to disappear in the successor era as party trumped region everywhere (Table C.5.A).

Civil rights brought what was in most senses a more extreme version of the same story (Table C.5.B). In the opening period, region clearly trumped party, a difference exaggerated among Democrats but present for Republicans too. The diagnostic result was that Northern Republicans were more liberal not just than Southern Republicans but also than Southern Democrats. Yet as impressive as this opening divide was, underpinning the policy difference that more or less *defined* political regionalism for observers at the time, the first postwar period was also the last hurrah for an aggregate division on civil rights that could probably have been traced for more than a hundred years, had there been polling data to trace it.

With social welfare, a residual regional influence had simply collapsed in the successor era. With civil rights, party overcame region in this same period, with both Democratic Parties now on the left and both Republican Parties on the right. Yet region survived as a structuring influence inside those parties, with their Northern branches more liberal and their Southern branches more conservative. Patterned regional differences would finally collapse in the modern era, in a historically unprecedented fashion: Southern Republicans remained modestly right of Northern Republicans on civil rights, but Southern Democrats, the great original dissident cohort, ended up modestly *left* of their Northern counterparts.

Remarkably, national security managed to tell a regional story opposite to both social welfare and civil rights (Table C.5.C). Beginning with the smallest

Table C.5 **Region versus Party: Policy Alignments across Time**

	1. Social Welfare				2. Civil Rights				
	ND	*SD*	*NR*	*SR*	*ND*	*SD*	*NR*	*SR*	
Era 3	−.24	−.26	+.35	+.36	−.23	−.29	+.33	+.37	Era 3
Era 2	−.24	−.22	+.25	+.29	−.22	−.11	+.17	+.29	Era 2
Era 1	−.21	−.05	+.24	+.25	−.19	+.18	+.08	+.33	Era 1
	3. National Security				4. Cultural Values				
	ND	*SD*	*NR*	*SR*	*ND*	*SD*	*NR*	*SR*	
Era 3	−.26	−.11	+.28	+.36	−.23	−.07	+.19	+.26	Era 3
Era 2	−.19	+.01	+.11	+.22	−.13	+.07	+.04	+.14	Era 2
Era 1	−.03	+.02	+.01	+.00	−.07	+.08	+.02	+.17	Era 1

regional impact in the opening period, it was the policy domain with the smallest party impact as well. Ironically, when national security came into partisan alignment in the successor era, it acquired a strong regional alignment too. So the domain that had rendered both organizing principles trivial in the opening period became the one where the two were most equally engaged. Only the modern era would see party clearly trump region as an aligning influence on national security, though the North-South divide would retain a serious secondary influence, with the South leaning clearly to the right inside both parties.

The domain that resisted alignment by party attachment the longest, however, was cultural values, where the continuing ability of geographic region to shape cultural preferences buttressed this continuing resistance (Table C.5.D). In the opening period, region dominated party to the point where, as with civil rights, Southern Democrats were right of Northern Republicans. Yet unlike the situation in the three other policy domains, this cultural alignment would be essentially unchanged in the successor era. Northern Democrats were still the only cultural liberals; Southern Democrats were still right of Northern Republicans. Only in the modern world did party finally overcome region as an aligning influence for cultural values.

In this world, Democrats were on the left and Republicans on the right for cultural values in both regions, an ordering that embodied the triumph of party attachment. In order for this to happen, Southern Democrats had to move noticeably to the left, all the way across the ideological center from conservative to liberal, just as Northern Republicans had to move notably to the right, abandoning a long-standing cultural moderation. In the event, both did, though a secondary regional deviation did remain substantial inside the Democratic Party, where Southern Democrats, only slightly left of the national average, were still impressively moderate by comparison to the three other regionalized parties.

That is a story of growth in the impact of party attachment and decline in the impact of geographic region. Region began as the leading influence in more domains than party for the immediate postwar years, when party led only on social welfare. Yet party rose as an aligning influence within every domain across time, until it became the lead influence in all four. Because the increasing dominance of party went hand in hand with an overall convergence of partisan alignments across policy domains, the decline of region inevitably accompanied this result. That said, the comparative evolutionary story was not linear in any simple sense. Region actually gained influence in the security domain after the immediate postwar years, while it retained a major secondary influence on both national security and cultural values during the modern era.

In that light, Table C.6 returns to the ideological distance—the degree of partisan polarization—between aggregate Democrats and aggregate Republicans across the postwar period. Scores are now for four regional parties in the

Table C.6 Regional Alignments in a Unidimensional Politics: Policy Convergence Revisited

	A. SW and CR				B. SW and NS				C. SW and CV			
	ND	*SD*	*NR*	*SR*	*ND*	*SD*	*NR*	*SR*	*ND*	*SD*	*NR*	*SR*
Era 3	.01	.03	.02	.01	.02	.15	.07	.00	.01	.20	.10	.10
Era 2	.02	.11	.08	.00	.05	.23	.14	.07	.11	.15	.21	.15
Era 1	.02	.23	.16	.08	.18	.07	.23	.25	.14	.11	.22	.08

four major domains, taken from Table C.5. Entries in Table C.6 are then the differences between Northern Democrats on social welfare and Northern Democrats on civil rights (−.24 and −.23 = .01), Southern Democrats on social welfare and civil rights (−.26 and −.29 = .03), and so on through all four regional parties in all three available comparisons to social welfare.

Once again, the convergence of social welfare and civil rights is straightforward (Table C.6.A). Northern Democrats had aligned the two domains in parallel from the start, as had Southern Republicans. Northern Republicans and Southern Democrats began to bring the two domains together in the second postwar period, coming into full alignment for the modern era. It was Southern Democrats who had featured the greatest difference between the two domains in the opening period, being clearly conservative on civil rights but modestly liberal on social welfare. So the move toward a common national pattern required the most from these Southern Democrats, who became clearly liberal on social welfare but only moderately liberal on civil rights in the successor period, before they too moved to full convergence in the modern world.

National security would end up with a similar movement over time, albeit never as completely and by a different trajectory (Table C.6.B). The opening chapter in a story of ultimate convergence between social welfare and national security actually began with the Southern Democrats, the regional party showing the least difference between welfare and security alignments at the start. Yet when national security assumed a partisan alignment for the nation as a whole in the successor period, these Southern Democrats, remaining much more conservative on security issues than their Northern counterparts, were the ones who moved farthest away from the new pattern. By contrast, Northern Democrats moved into complete convergence with social welfare, while Southern Republicans moved strongly toward it. When Northern Republicans aligned their preferences on welfare and security in the modern world, that left Southern Democrats with the biggest remaining gap between the two domains.

Given that cultural values resisted alignment by party attachment for the longest time, retaining the greatest secondary influence by geographic region, it is hardly surprising that this fourth and final domain remained at the greatest distance from social welfare in its overall alignment through all the years after the Second World War (Table C.6.C). In the immediate postwar years, it was actually Northern Republicans who showed the greatest disjunction between public preferences on social welfare and cultural values, being far less conservative on culture than on welfare. In the second era, a move leftward by Northern Democrats when everyone else was essentially stable made Southern Democrats the farthest out of alignment with a national pattern, though no one was really moving toward convergence in a substantial way.

Northern Democrats did ultimately come into full convergence across all four domains, including cultural values, though what this did was to make them the exception among four regionalized parties, where Southern Democrats followed the opposite trajectory. Their conservative cultural preferences had actually been only minimally distant from their welfare preferences in the opening years, but they did not move toward cultural convergence when they began to converge on social welfare in the successor era, and they were to move only farther away in the modern world. Lastly, the two regional Republican Parties, Northern and Southern, while they moved clearly toward convergence in the modern world, still had their greatest distance from a welfare alignment in the domain of cultural values.

In the end, then, convergence between social welfare and civil rights was to be powerful and homogeneous across parties and across regions. Convergence between social welfare and national security would be similarly strong, but with a remaining dissidence among Southern Democrats, a population considerably more liberal on social welfare than on national security. And cultural values, despite seeing party displace region as its dominant organizing principle, retained the greatest difference between the two alignments, a cultural tension that was generalized to three of the four regional parties. So once again, cultural values stood out as the great alternative to social welfare, the policy domain that most strongly resisted the increasingly consensual welfare template.

Social Alternatives to Partisan Alignment

As between the two contending grand principles for organizing policy alignments, party attachment was broadly and increasingly ascendant, while geographic region was broadly and simultaneously in retreat. But was the rise of party likewise accompanied by a decline in the organizing power of basic social cleavages? Alternatively, did the decline of region open opportunities for the various cleavages to increase their own organizing power? Or—a third alternative suggested by the loose connection between the rise of party and the decline of region—did key social cleavages chart idiosyncratic paths, providing differential contributions to (or constraints on) the convergence of partisan alignments across policy domains?

Social welfare can provide only a truncated test of these alternative evolutionary possibilities (Table C.7). Region was already gone as a dominant aligning influence for social welfare in the immediate postwar years, which meant that the links between class membership and welfare preferences were the crucial input to a partisan alignment—an implicit template—that could be used to track partisan convergence and ultimately to unpack a common evolution across the big four policy domains. By subtraction, if region was gone, the evolutionary story for social welfare had to follow from (and depend on) the aligning powers of party attachment plus social class. So an analysis of their joint evolution has to begin with a look at the inherent contributions of class membership to policy alignment in the absence of party attachment.

Analyzed this way, with class as a direct influence on welfare preferences, two central points emerge (Table C.7.A). In the first, a class alignment on welfare preferences was consistent across all three postwar eras, running left to right from lower to upper classes while expanding across the period as a whole. So the rise of party obviously coexisted with a rise in the aligning power of class membership. Yet in the other central point, an implicit alliance between the lower and middle classes against the upper class in the immediate postwar years would disappear in the second period and stay gone in the third. In its place, the middle class was to become a kind of "swing preference" between upper and lower classes. By this light too, social class was not in conflict with—much less repressed by—a growing influence for party attachment.

Table C.7 **Policy Alignments and Social Class: Social Welfare across Time**

A. Policy Preferences by Class: A Stable Cleavage

	Low	Mid	High	
Era 3	−.17	+.02	+.16	Era 3
Era 2	−.22	+.01	+.14	Era 2
Era 1	−.11	−.05	+.12	Era 1

B. Joint Policy Preferences by Party and Class: Instantiation and Persistence

	Dems			Reps			
	Low	Mid	High	Low	Mid	High	
Era 3	−.31	−.23	−.17	+.16	+.38	+.44	Era 3
Era 2	−.39	−.20	−.11	+.10	+.25	+.34	Era 2
Era 1	−.24	−.18	−.09	+.11	+.15	+.38	Era 1

Considering party and class jointly adds nuance to this story but does nothing to upend those class-based results (Table C.7.B). The generic impact of social class on welfare preferences also ran regularly inside both parties, again left to right from lower to middle to upper classes, though it did not increase much within those parties. Rather, the key difference was *within classes by party*, confirming a greater impact on policy alignment by party attachment rather than by social class. The one further individual twist worth noting came among middle-class Republicans, who changed their welfare preferences the most across the postwar years. But the bottom line remained that all six partisan cohorts as isolated by class remained in a neat, regular, and stable alignment across all three eras. Class was neither replaced nor reduced within a growing alignment by party.

Racial background offered the deepest social cleavage available to compete with party or region, though also the one most narrowly focused within the larger society. Civil rights was—and would remain—the policy domain registering the influence of race most directly, where a huge racial divide on rights policy was already evident in the first postwar period (Table C.8.A). Yet the practical impact of such a deep but focused cleavage would be shaped in major ways by the rise of party, the decline of region, and, most of all, a reconstruction of the electorate that was in effect the formal reconstitution of the political community.

Further rolling adjustments within this community would then become the ongoing story of partisan alignments on civil rights. In the immediate postwar years, region trumped party as an organizing influence for policy preferences on civil rights, with the two Southern parties, Democratic and Republican, well to the right of their Northern counterparts. Race possessed independent aligning power even in these early years, but this was limited by the small size of the black electorate (Table C.8.B). Yet in the years leading into the successor period, there was major electoral reform, aimed most centrally at (re)enfranchising black Americans, and it was to be strikingly successful. The black electorate doubled in this second era, then added a further 50% in the modern era, in effect tripling its share of the electorate from the opening period. The rise of party, coupled with this major alteration in the formal composition of the electorate, would push the aligning power of region into the background in the second postwar period, while bringing the comparative organizing power of party and race into a subsequent—and lasting—dialogue (Table C.8.C). There were nearly no black Republicans, before or after enfranchisement, so the relevant cohorts for following this dialogue were black Democrats, nonblack Democrats, and (all) Republicans. Among them, blacks would be more liberal than nonblacks quite apart from party, while Democrats would be more liberal than Republicans quite apart from race.

Table C.8 **Policy Alignments and Racial Background: Civil Rights across Time**

	A. Policy Preferences by Race: A Stable Chasm		B. Black Vote Share: A Changing Electorate	
	Black	Non-Bl	% Black	
Era 3	−.68	+.13	15%	Era 3
Era 2	−.98	+.10	10%	Era 2
Era 1	−.82	+.05	5%	Era 1

C. Joint Policy Preferences by Party and Race: An Enduring Difference in a Polarizing World

	Black Dems	Non-Bl Dems	All Reps
Era 3	−.69	−.12	+.36
Era 2	−.98	+.00	+.19
Era 1	−.83	−.00	+.12

Yet racial background and not party attachment still dominated the resulting composite. Partisan polarization among nonblacks did expand, nearly quadrupling by the modern era. But the racial difference among Democrats would remain larger than any partisan difference within races where civil rights was concerned. So unlike social welfare, with which civil rights would relentlessly converge, the key social cleavage in the latter domain continued to dominate party attachment, even as the parties became more clearly divided on rights policy.

Given that policy preferences on civil rights were the ones most strongly organized by geographic region at the start, and given that the South possessed the largest potential black electorate but also the greatest prior minimization of its vote, it is unsurprising that the South would tell a more extreme regional substory. Black enfranchisement did help bring the South into general alignment with the nation on civil rights in the second postwar era. Yet this remained largely a black story, that is, a simple story of augmented numbers. Not until the third period did nonblack Southern Democrats come into line with the national pattern, though when they did, the result was historically unprecedented: Southern Democrats, long the aggressive dissidents on civil rights, were now more liberal in their rights preferences than their Northern counterparts.

A student of the political role of the great religions might have been excused during the immediate postwar years for believing that religious denomination was the major social cleavage with no serious role in generating partisan

Cultural values would ultimately be the policy domain that best captured a growing political importance for the great denominational families, but in this opening period, four of the five denominations with a serious presence in American society were roughly clustered in their cultural preferences, while the lone dissident family, the Others, was dwarfed by the three largest (Era 1 in Table C.9.A). At the same time, region not only dominated party as an aligning influence for cultural values but also crushed out the small distinction between the two denominations with a serious presence in both major regions, namely the Mainstreams and the Evangelicals, converting modest apparent differences into regional artifacts.

And the same summary could be extended into the successor era: region dominating party, denominations differing little, remaining differences largely a regional artifact (Era 2 in Table C.9.A). With hindsight, there were incipient developments in this second postwar era whose relevance would become clear in

Table C.9 **Policy Alignments and Religious Denomination: Cultural Values across Time**

A. Policy Preferences by Denomination: Religious Anchors

	EP	MP	C	BE	O	
Era 3	+.24	.00	−.04	−.04	−.26	Era 3
Era 2	+.18	−.02	+.03	+.01	−.36	Era 2
Era 1	+.08	+.02	+.01	−.04	−.30	Era 1

B. Policy Preferences by Party and Denomination: Partisan Mobilization Appears

	1. Dems					2. Reps				
	O	MP	C	BE	EP	O	C	MP	EP	BE
Era 3	−.40	−.20	−.14	−.05	−.01	+.04	+.11	+.18	+.38	*
Era 2	−.46	−.09	−.01	−.01	+.15	−.16	+.09	+.02	+.21	*
Era 1	−.36	−.08	+.01	−.02	+.06	−.14	+.01	+.09	+.08	*

C. The Changing Religious Landscape, Era 1 to Era 3

	1. All	2. Dem	3. Reps
EP	+10%	+ 3%	+21%
MP	−14%	−7%	−26%
C	−10%	−16%	−1%
O	+7%	+8%	+6%
BE	+7%	+12%	*

* Negligible presence.

the modern world, when their influence became diagnostic. The lesser of these, albeit the one that might have been most easily noticed, was a clear move to the cultural right by Evangelical Protestants. The larger of the two, but also the one that could be observed only after the fact, was the emergence of another major engine of political change. This was *partisan mobilization*, the infusion of party politics into previously neutral social cleavages. When it appeared decisively in the modern era, everything would change (Era 3 in Table C.9.A).

At that point, party came to dominate region for policy alignments on cultural values, while a new and powerful interaction between party and denomination reduced region to even a tertiary influence only among Evangelical Protestants in the South. Very little changed in the aggregate preferences of the major religious families, but the impact of party inside denomination exploded, as expressed through the ideological distance between partisan pieces: +.38 (Republican) versus –.01 (Democratic) among Evangelicals, +.18 versus –.20 among Mainstreams, +.11 versus –.14 among Catholics, and +.04 versus –.40 among the Others.[8] So if party surpassed denomination in shaping policy alignments, denomination located the result within parties: Evangelicals on the right, Others on the left, and Catholics and Mainstreams in between.

Religious denomination would go on to make a second, largely autonomous contribution to partisan alignments by way of differential growth. In the beginning, Mainstreams and Catholics dominated the religious landscape (Table C.9.C). By the modern era, the growth sectors were instead the Evangelicals (black and nonblack) plus the Others. Moreover, two of the growing denominations were the ones at the ideological extremes, while the declining denominations were the ones that had once energized the ideological center. In passing, the parties were effectively reconstituted. The Democrats shed Catholics but gained black Evangelicals (Table C.9.C.2). The Republicans shed Mainstream Protestants but surged among their (nonblack) Evangelical brethren. So while partisanship was being injected into previously nonpartisan denominations, their newly partisan pieces were growing or shrinking as major secondary contributions to partisan alignments.

Sex is the fourth and last of the major social cleavages, but unlike the other three, its relationship to policy preferences was distinguished by weakness at the start and instability across time. Its expected marker domain was most often conceived to be national security, and in the immediate postwar years, men were indeed hawkish and women dovish (Table C.10.A). Yet even this marker would vary, falling away in the second period before surging back in the third. And the other domains were capable of equally impressive variation, as exemplified by cultural values that opened with men liberal and women conservative, fell essentially to zero in the successor period, then reversed ideological direction with men conservative and women liberal for the modern world.

Conclusion

Table C.10 **Policy Alignments and Sex: National Security across Time**

A. National Security across Time: A Variable Cleavage in a Variable Domain

	Women	*Men*	
Era 3	−.08	+.12	Era 3
Era 2	−.01	+.00	Era 2
Era 1	−.03	+.04	Era 1

B. A Changing Party Balance: Parties within Sexes

		Men	*Women*
Era 1, 1952–1968	Dems	48%	52%
	Reps	45%	55%
Era 3, 1992–2008	Dems	40%	60%
	Reps	51%	49%

C. A Changing Party Balance: Sexes within Parties

		DRFs	*RRFs*
Era 1, 1952–1968	Men	62%	38%
	Women	60%	40%
Era 3, 1992–2008	Men	51%	49%
	Women	62%	38%

Those were not policy linkages to buttress stable alignments, while interacting them with party attachment plus geographic region only magnifies a picture of idiosyncratic connections across time (see Chapter 4). Yet if that is not a situation parallel to the links between class and welfare, race and rights, or religion and culture, the four wandering divisions between men and women by policy domain were associated with a major and consistent change, in overall *party balance,* a change that was arguably larger than the relationship between individual social cleavages and specific policy domains. Or at least, the ability to widen the gap between party attachments by men versus women had to shape the partisan alignments characterizing social welfare, civil rights, cultural values, and, of course, national security.

A basic difference in the party attachments of men versus women was recognized early, then tracked through a focus on this "gender gap" (Table C.10.B). The gap itself rose from 3% in the first postwar era, when men were slightly more Democratic and women slightly more Republican, to 11% in the modern world, when party loyalties by sex had reversed. At a minimum, change on that scale confirmed that sex could expand its influence, while party attachment did the same. Yet the crucial aspect of these changes, and their critical impacts on partisan alignment, were partially obscured by this initial focus. Looked at the other way around—sexes by party rather than parties by sex—it becomes clear that Republican gains among men were substantially larger than Democratic gains among women, more than twice as large in fact (Table C.10.C).

So a growing gap between men and women in their party attachments was not politically neutral. It contributed to a shift in party balance toward the Republican Party. Seen this way too, sex was capable of expanding its influence, while party attachment did the same. But seen this second way, sex contributed a noteworthy shift across time, with an influence on partisan politics that was not dependent on any single policy domain. This impact could be lost by insisting that an effective social cleavage *should* operate consistently among its internal categories across time. What sex argued instead was that men and women could be moved by very different policy domains, at different points in time—as indeed they were. Republican women who switched to the Democratic Party were incentivized both early and late by policy dissidence on social welfare, just as Democratic men who switched to the Republican Party, largely in the modern world, were incentivized instead by policy dissidence on cultural values, national security, and civil rights.

The Roots of Political Conflict

In the end, that is a comprehensive story of the social roots of political conflicts, the conflicts central to American politics since the end of World War II. The seedbeds for that story are four major social cleavages, namely social class, racial background, religious denomination, and sex. They generate the policy preferences characterizing the four major policy domains of this postwar politics, namely social welfare, civil rights, cultural values, and national security. The links between social cleavages and policy preferences are then picked up and institutionalized by the political parties, becoming embedded in party attachments, though parties have considerable autonomy over when and how to respond, both of which can be further shaped by party structure, especially the distinction between the active party and its rank and file.

What results are a set of partisan alignments linking social cleavages, policy preferences, and party attachments. In turn, these alignments become the main analytic tool for isolating and following *change* in postwar politics. In the process, they highlight four change engines, namely instantiation, enfranchisement, mobilization, and individual (re)alignment. Ultimately, these partisan alignments are rooted in a large and diverse general public. Ultimately, they go on to provide the contours of programmatic disputes inside government. They do this year in and year out. In some fundamental sense, they are the structure of American politics in their time, remembering that "structure" hardly implies permanence. Partisan alignments for the four major policy domains, as well as all four alignments at different points in time, can (and do) shuffle their influences as they converge with—or cross-cut—each other.

Social Welfare

Any effort to elicit that structure, and especially any attempt to summarize the result, has to begin with the policy domain and the social cleavage that were to be at the heart of partisan alignments across the entire postwar period. The domain is social welfare; the associated cleavage is social class. The Great Depression brought welfare preferences to the center of American politics, while the coming of an extended welfare state gave this policy domain an obvious and continuing programmatic focus. In what was something of a grand historical accident—Herbert Hoover was not opposed to the use of government in economic recovery, while Franklin Roosevelt flirted with budget cutting in his electoral campaign—the Democrats became the party of the welfare state, and the Republicans the party of limitation, revision, and resistance.

From the start, these welfare preferences were neatly aligned by class, being liberal on the bottom, moderate in the middle, and conservative at the top. This was true for society as a whole, regardless of party attachment. Yet it was also true inside both major parties, where the resulting array was again regular and unfailing. Party did dominate class in the sense that Democratic identifiers in all classes were left of Republican identifiers in all classes. But both principles were regularly and systematically at work in a continuum that ran from lower-class Democrats on the left to upper-class Republicans on the right with every class-and-party combination in its appropriate place in between. So the result was an evolving set of partisan alignments, underpinned in a remarkably regular and patterned way by social class.

In the immediate postwar years, it was still reasonable to believe that the class cleavage could actually recede as an organizing influence, either as welfare politics returned to a noncrisis mode or as other policy concerns became more insistent, implicitly elbowing social welfare aside. In a similar manner, the neat and reliable patterning to the link between class and welfare preferences hardly came with a guarantee of some neat and regular trajectory, linear across time and symmetric by party. But the real roadblock to the instantiation of these immediate postwar arrangements was the revival of geographic region, the great alternative to party attachment as an organizing principle for policy alignments.

So the aligning power of region was what had to be overcome if these opening relationships among welfare preferences, social classes, and party attachments were to be instantiated rather than undone. Political region was in turn embodied most centrally in the long-standing North/South divide. In truth, the Republican Party had already reached a kind of regional convergence on welfare policy, but the Democratic Party still possessed two distinctly regional pieces, where the Southern Democratic piece was often the ideological fulcrum for welfare legislation, being more conservative than its Northern Democratic counterpart but more liberal than national Republicans.

Moreover, this regional dissidence had distinctive class underpinnings of its own inside the Democratic Party. In this, the Southern Democrats privileged their upper-class identifiers far more than Northern Democrats did, though region augmented this class effect by producing upper-class Southerners who were far more conservative than upper-class Northern counterparts. On the one hand, social class was clearly on the rise as an aligning principle for American politics; that was an initial legacy of the New Deal. On the other hand, economic welfare as a policy concern had hardly been absent in the years before the coming of the New Deal and its welfare state, when policy preferences had largely been expressed through support for the various regional economies rather than through generic social classes.

This far-reaching regional difference, by party and by class, was what would come apart in the successor period, when it was superseded by party attachment. Its undoing would, in turn, have two distinct pieces. A large part of the corrective would come from the enfranchisement of black Southerners, altering the social composition of the Southern Democratic Party, about which more later. But an equally major if more amorphous contribution came from the confirmed instantiation of social welfare during the preceding period, as the leading policy difference between the two parties nationwide. This made those economically conservative upper-class Southern Democrats increasingly and inescapably out of place in their traditional party home, though only time could make this new partisan alignment for social welfare both stable and diagnostic.

Yet social welfare as a substantive domain, social class as an ongoing cleavage, and their joint links to party attachment were to remain sufficiently important to the voting public and sufficiently adaptive to changing programmatic needs as to allow the initial aligning pattern not just to continue but actually to grow. There could still be important variations across time. In the second postwar period, this welfare division was augmented by a strong move to the left by the Democratic Party, while the Republicans largely marked time. In the successor period, our modern era, an augmented welfare division came instead from a strong move to the right by the Republican Party, while the Democrats largely stayed in place. But the bottom line was that social welfare continued to expand its shaping influence on the partisan alignments of American politics.

Racial Background

Civil rights as a policy domain in the opening postwar years produced what might have been viewed as a pale version of this welfare alignment, clear enough to suggest that the rights domain might ultimately join social welfare in a common array but weak enough to be a forerunner to nearly any alternative evolution. A gifted observer might have gone on to recognize these early years as a key period of societal ferment on rights issues. Yet this was more inescapably a period when the Democratic Party contained both the main active proponents and the main active opposition to major policy change in the rights domain. Gifted with hindsight, we can look back and see that racial background was already the dominant social cleavage for public preferences on civil rights. That would never change. But at the time and more directly, this meant a restricted black minority that was strongly cathected by the issue, coupled with a far larger nonblack majority that was largely indifferent in the aggregate.

The successor period would make it all look different. In policy terms, there would be a veritable civil rights revolution. In political terms, there would be an increasing alignment of right preferences with party attachment, Democrats to the left and Republicans to the right, leading to substantial shifts on both sides. Along the way, there would be a clear diminution of the major regional divergence characterizing these early alignments. Yet at the center of this whole cluster of developments would be one of the major change engines in all of postwar politics, namely voter enfranchisement. A formal redefinition of the political community would be what principally drove changing partisan alignments on civil rights, directly by way of additions to the electorate but also secondarily though the huge array of mutual adjustments that had to follow.

Yet unlike the situation on social welfare, where party continued to be buttressed by social class but began and remained the dominant influence on policy alignments, the key cleavage for civil rights, namely racial background, would begin as far more closely connected to policy alignments and continue to dominate party as an aligning influence, even as the shaping role of party expanded. Moreover, even more than with social welfare, this relationship between racial background and policy attachment on rights issues had a major regional aspect, since the black population was disproportionately located in the American South, where Southern Democrats, along with the residue of an old Southern Republican Party, began the postwar period as the conservatives on rights policy within the nation as a whole.

Programmatically hesitant about social welfare, Southern Democrats were aggressively dissident on civil rights. The (re)enfranchisement of black Southerners, together with the instantiation of social welfare as the dominant policy divide for party politics in the nation as a whole, moved the South to the left on both civil rights and social welfare in this second postwar period. Because black Southerners were always on the left in both domains, what they would contribute additionally was thus their augmented aggregate numbers. Yet where nonblack Southerners joined the national Democratic position on social welfare in this second period, they would make the same move on civil rights only in the modern era, though they would make it at that point. So regional closure was essentially complete for social welfare in the second postwar era, and fully complete on civil rights only in the third.

Within this change, the difference between nonblack Democrats and the Republicans would expand as time passed, though the difference between races would remain stronger, even inside the Democratic Party. Still, the largest single impact of voter enfranchisement remained the doubling of the black share of the electorate in the second postwar period, with a further increase sufficient to triple that original share in the successor period. More than with any other social cleavage, the resulting impacts on partisan alignment were impelled not by changes in the link between social cleavage and policy preference, as with social welfare, nor by the partisan elevation of previously apolitical preferences, much more the story of religious denominations (below), but rather by formal alterations in the bounds of the political community, courtesy of voter enfranchisement, along with the rolling ramifications and adjustments that followed.

Religious Denomination

The immediate postwar years were a quiet—even quiescent—period for policy conflicts stemming from cultural values. In the long runup to the Great Depression, these conflicts had been an important aspect of party attachment. In a sense, the New Deal put the last of them to sleep when it repealed Prohibition, long a central focus of cultural disputes in American society. The New Deal was then followed by World War II, where concerns for national security, not cultural policy, came to the fore. Afterward, commentators noted a desire for national unity and a return to "normalcy" as defining features of American society in the immediate postwar years.

Not only were cultural values unaligned by party attachment in that environment, but they were also close to unaligned by religious denomination, the social cleavage previously most connected to them. A small cadre of religious Others was strikingly dissident from the three great religious families, namely

Mainstream Protestants, Evangelical Protestants, and Catholics, but these three were clustered near the national average. Such a balance lacked the statistical makings of denominational conflict, while different issues—the proper composition of the welfare state, the proper pursuit of a Cold War, an incipient civil rights revolution—were more than enough to absorb the national policy agenda in the absence of pressing cultural conflicts.

Only hindsight would suggest that the successor period was sufficiently different either to begin bringing cultural issues back to the center of American politics or to register their independent rise. With hindsight, on the other hand, we can see two developments that would be harbingers of something very different by the modern era. The first was a solid move to the right on cultural values by the Evangelical Protestants. This move was harder to discern if Evangelicals were treated as a conglomerate, rather than distinguishing black Evangelicals as a separate denomination. On the other hand, if this is done retrospectively, an autonomous Evangelical move to the right becomes considerably more impressive.

This move was in turn part of a second development, gathering two subtrends that would explode in the third postwar period. First among these was the incipient arrival of denominational partisanship, that is, the infusion of party politics *inside* the major denominations for all of the great religious families except black Evangelicals, who had too few Republican members for partisanship to matter. Already under way among (nonblack) Evangelicals by the second postwar period, partisan mobilization would reach into the other major mobilizations in a serious fashion by the modern world, while beneath these individual polarizations was a second major trend, easier to observe but harder to connect to politics as it was unfolding.

This involved the numerical growth or decline of the denominations themselves, in a fashion destined to exacerbate cultural conflict. The growth populations were the two culturally extreme denominations, the Evangelicals for cultural conservatives and the Others for cultural liberals. The declining populations were the major culturally centrist denominations, the Mainstream Protestants and the Catholics. So both growth and decline fed into the impact of a generalized partisan infusion. In that sense, party attachment ultimately dominated social cleavage. Yet the inherent conservatism, moderation, or liberalism of the denominations remained an important secondary influence on the ideological alignment of cultural values.

In the opening years, there had been an important regional character to the distribution of these denominations as well. Evangelicals, black as well as nonblack, were concentrated in the South, while Catholics were concentrated in the North. Only the Mainstreams, destined for the most severe contraction across the postwar period, were well represented in both regions. But since there had been little difference among the big three denominations in their cultural preferences, and very unlike the situation for civil rights, this regional distribution did not matter much, while by the time partisan mobilization had arrived within all the major denominations that had a serious presence in both parties, it was this partisan infusion, not the distribution of denominations by region, that mattered politically.

Sex

The great policy domain that did not feature so much as a nascent hint of partisan alignment in the opening postwar years was national security, though the reasons for the absence of such an alignment were more or less precisely opposite to the reasons for its absence on cultural values. Judged by its programmatic impact, national security certainly rivaled social welfare as the crucial domain for policy conflict during this first postwar period. Rather than being put back to sleep as a matter of political contestation by the end of World War II, security issues were re-emphasized by the subsequent appearance of an international Cold War, one in which the United States would play a leading role from the start.

So where a yearning for normalcy was the backdrop to cultural preferences in these immediate postwar years, an actual "hot" war in Korea, with a major commitment of American forces and a major loss of American lives, was the backdrop to national security. Yet the resultant division of hawks versus doves still showed no relationship to party attachment. Indeed, national security was the lone policy domain where the last of the major social cleavages, namely sex, was actually stronger than party attachment in aligning policy preferences. On the other hand, and unlike the relationships between social class and social welfare, racial background and civil rights, or religious denomination and cultural values, this link between sex and national security would prove unstable, falling all the way to zero in the successor period, then rebounding to outdistance the other three domains in the modern era.

That marked an especially volatile relationship, though if the focus was sex as an aligning principle, two of the other three major domains would be very labile as well, each in its own way. Social welfare would show a modest regular increase in the organizing power of sex, even as party attachment would begin stronger and grow faster. Civil rights would follow the opposite trajectory, showing a small initial relationship by sex that was to disappear in the second postwar period and stay gone in the third. And cultural values, while modestly connected to sex at the start, would actually reverse directions, with men liberal and women conservative at the start, morphing into a modern world where women were liberal and men conservative.

On the surface, this suggested an extremely limited ability for differences between men and women to shape partisan alignments. Yet sex was to differ from the other major cleavages in an important operational way, one even more directly connected to partisan alignments despite these wobbly relationships to policy preference. Sex was to be associated with—indeed, it appeared to produce—a major shift in *party balance* for the nation as a whole. The statistical impact was clear enough. In the beginning, men were slightly more Democratic and women slightly more Republican. By the modern era, women were considerably more Democratic, while men had shifted even more heavily toward the Republicans. Together, the two sexes inevitably adjusted the overall party balance in society as they shifted.

So sex would be different from class, race, and religion in having less systematic links to party attachment by way of policy preferences, yet simultaneously play a serious role in shaping the balance of party identifiers within all four partisan alignments. But more to the explicitly political point, this evolution— women toward the Democrats and men toward the Republicans—would not result in a reciprocal exchange. The size of the move among men was considerably larger than the size of the move among women, so that a national party balance moved simultaneously in the direction of the Republicans. This was why a collection of wobbly relationships between sex and policy preference did not have to net out to a wash for the resulting partisan alignments.

Instead, a focus on party *switching* by sex highlighted the policy realms where men or women—separately, it did not have to be both men and women—were most out of line with their own active parties, and thus had the greatest incentives to defect. Indeed, the critical policy domains for party switching, isolated by sex, were most definitely not the same for men versus women:

- Republican women were the partisan population that shifted most notably toward the Democrats over time, while among these Republican women, social welfare was clearly the domain where the median woman was most out of alignment with her own active party, and thus most subject to cross-pressures from policy wishes.
- Democratic men were a partisan population that shifted even more strongly toward the Republicans across the postwar years, but among these Democratic men, there were actually three dissident domains where the median man was most out of alignment with his active party, namely national security, civil rights, and cultural values.
- As a result, social welfare among women and all three other domains among men were policy realms that generated major incentives for party switching, and while most voters, female or male, did not switch, the aggregate of

individual moves by sex would nevertheless drive a substantial change in overall party balance for the nation as a whole.

A Concluding Note

In the end, that is a picture of changing policy conflicts across the postwar world, a picture developed from systematic data, broken down by policy preference, social cleavage, and party attachment before being reassembled into partisan alignments. This composite picture gathers all the great realms for policy conflict, namely social welfare, civil rights, national security, and cultural values. It encompasses the social cleavages that give rise to preferences within those realms, namely social class, racial background, religious denomination, and sex. And it situates the link between social cleavages and policy preferences in the nature of their attachment to political parties, an attachment that was largely responsible for converting those links into institutionalized and ongoing political conflicts.

Those conflicts, along with the associated policy positions on them, were readily recognizable by political commentators as well as the general public, just as their social roots, along with the crucial transmission process for socially rooted preferences, were ordinarily lost from view—and all too often lost from political analyses. Yet for many purposes these links between social cleavages and policy preferences, along with a regularized transmission into party attachment, captured ultimately in partisan alignments, are nothing less than the (changing) structure of American politics. "Structure" implies that no one—not individual office holders, not organized political parties, not even a general public—could simply *decide* on how those factors should work. Yet change in these alignments is an equally important part of the story, where policy instantiation, voter enfranchisement, partisan mobilization, and individual realignment were working constantly to reshape this structure.

Afterword

PARTISAN ALIGNMENTS, VOTER PRIORITIES, AND PRESIDENTIAL BALLOTS

In the end, that is a comprehensive story of the social roots of political conflicts, of the links between those roots and policy preferences, and of the way that party attachment did (or did not) institutionalize those links to make them the ongoing substance of American politics. What carries this story are the *partisan alignments* that appear and evolve, ultimately drawn into a pattern common to all major policy domains while retaining individual, largely social, differences among them. These dozen partisan alignments, from four policy domains for three temporal eras, are what add up to a comprehensive picture of the roots and evolution of postwar political conflict.

The alignments themselves are a product of the preferences of a large and diverse public, while at the same time, they constitute the backdrop to programmatic conflicts inside the institutions of government. They do this year in and year out. In that sense, they summarize—they are—critical elements of the structure of American politics in their time. So one would expect that these partisan alignments must also be integral to electoral politics. After all, they simultaneously constitute the larger context within which any election campaign is conducted. Yet isolating their influence on voting behavior is not a simple and straightforward process, containing as it does a trio of analytic minefields.

The first is just the fact that any given election is but a single sample of an extended period, dominated by an inherited background, yes, but mixed with candidate characteristics, issues of the day, plus fads, fashions, and idiosyncrasies. Yet there are two further analytic challenges that cannot be sidestepped merely by attending to multiple elections. One is intrinsic and recurrent: the voting influence of partisan alignments is hard to isolate because they are so deeply integral to the vote itself. The other is more the product of voting analyses with too narrow a focus, by analysts who fail to acknowledge the shaping context within which their analyses unfold.

To begin at the beginning: individuals have social roots, which produce policy preferences, which are captured by political parties, which at least in our time have moved farther and farther apart ideologically. This alone is sufficient to encourage a growing share of Democrats to vote Democratic and of Republicans to vote Republican, as they increasingly do. In that sense, partisan alignments are recurrently and increasingly instantiated in the vote itself, long before it has candidates, long before they have strategies, and long before these produce an election campaign. For candidates, one idiosyncratic outcome can still be everything. Yet for analysts, the relevant political conflicts of an era, the public preferences on them that emerge in conjunction with social cleavages, and the connection of those links to party attachment do not *cause* an individual vote. Rather, the two sides of that particular equation—partisan alignments and voting behavior—are effectively identities.

By extension, many otherwise careful voting analyses are tautological, their inputs and their outputs being essentially the same—that is, to go all the way back to Chapter 1, why an analysis which is not artifactual must go in search of the social roots of political conflict. On the other hand, and this is the good news, stating the problem this way goes some distance toward generating a solution. Or at least, there are important aspects of voting behavior—perhaps the aspects most important to candidates—that have the ability in principle to circumvent the problem. These involve asking about the propensity to *escape from* overarching partisan alignments, in this case by voting contrary to its ongoing influences. What this requires, though the requirement itself has become more challenging in our time, is sufficient diversity of social backgrounds and policy preferences to provide a mix of incentives for supporting versus deviating from what would otherwise be the (previously established) logic of party attachment.

In simple terms, this approach merely formulates the question the other way around, asking which policy domains had the strongest impact on *dissident* voter choice, that is, on the tendency to vote Democratic among Republicans or Republican among Democrats. Analysis is then comparatively straightforward, with one huge cautionary alert. Once policy domains have come into a partisan alignment, and especially once that alignment begins to polarize, *every* domain will show a positive connection to party attachment when examined only on its own terms—which is where the second common failing emerges. To state the problem concretely: in the absence of the three other major policy domains, each and every one will show up as related not just to the vote but to voter dissidence if these domains are treated individually—even if they made no contribution at all when considered in the company of other, effectively dominant, policy domains.

AFTERWORD

So there is a necessary second element in searching, not for the marginal effect on the vote of a change in policy preferences in any given domain, but for the domains with the largest marginal impact—the true policy drivers—in a world where all four major domains are always simultaneously but often superficially present. The good news is that this problem is far easier to address than the one that follows from having partisan alignments that are inherent to the vote. The appropriate response to this second problem merely requires keeping all four major domains in the analysis whenever the goal is to see the impact of one or another domain in a context where its impact is not artifactual. The vast bulk of shaping influences by partisan alignments will still have occurred long before the ballot. But a crucial final impact can still be elicited by turning to voter behavior within the comprehensive context that the four together provide.

To that end, Figures A.1 through A.4 will gather the marginal effects of a one-point change in policy preferences with all four major domains in the analysis. In this way, "bogus" relationships—those that appear in one policy domain but are largely the result of another—can be removed from an examination of voting behavior. To that end, these figures must proceed through a simultaneous analysis of marginal effects: how much does the vote change in response to a change in preferences on social welfare, civil rights, national security, or cultural values, *while controlling for the other three*? Formally, the answers come from logit regressions of vote choice, providing a point estimate plus a confidence interval. Fortunately, as below, confidence intervals are small for most results, providing reassurance about the quality of their point estimates.

Marginal Effects for the Nation

Figure A.1 begins the picture of voter dissidence for each of the four major policy domains across three extended eras since the Second World War ended and the American National Election Study began. As a policy domain became organized by party attachment, it was conservative Democrats and liberal Republicans who acquired institutionalized incentives to defect to the other side, though whether they did so remained an empirical question, especially since voters could face incentives to move in opposite directions, given their own particular mix of policy preferences. So the degree of organization by party attachment and issue priorities among individual voters mattered, as did the share of partisans who were cross-pressured by any given combination of policy domains.

Seen this way, the immediate postwar years brought a simple and straightforward electoral environment (Era 1). Overwhelmingly, the main source of practical pressure to support a partisan candidate opposite to party attachment was social welfare (WW). Recall that welfare preferences were already and clearly

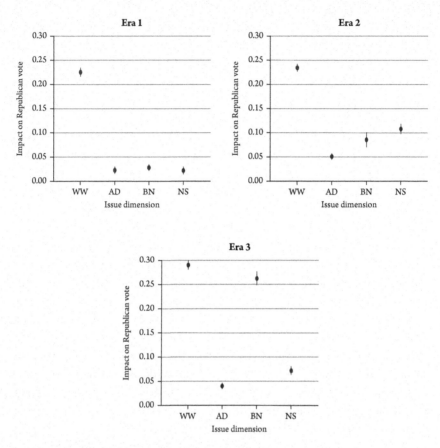

On the X-axis, WW stands for the domain of social welfare, AD for civil rights, BN for cultural values, and NS for national security.

Figure A.1 Marginal Effects Nationwide

On the x-axis, WW stands for the domain of social welfare, AD for civil rights, BN for cultural values, and NS for national security.

aligned with party, far more than any other domain. Yet the voting result confirms that there remained substantial populations whose preferences were out of sync with their party attachments, in the form of economically conservative Democrats and economically liberal Republicans—and these misalignments mattered. Overall, a one-point increase in welfare dissidence increased the probability of voting for the opposite party by 0.22.

By comparison, nothing else did. Civil rights (AD), cultural values (BN), and national security (NS) were all basically unaligned by party attachment. So it was hard to dub individual voters "out of sync" with their nominal party preferences if established party positions were largely exiguous in these other domains. Individual members of the general public did possess preferences that were liberal or conservative in these domains too, but those preferences could not systematically affect voting behavior if the parties did not differ programmatically on them. If this was the classic era of partisan alignment by welfare preference, then, social welfare was also the only domain that could seriously stress a prior party attachment, whether inherited from an earlier period or chosen through a contemporary mistake.

The successor era would repeat this dominance of social welfare at the same high level that had characterized the opening postwar years (Era 2). Yet a composite picture of voter priorities would become considerably more complex, since all three alternative domains came to life as voting influences. National security became the leading if still distant challenger to social welfare, in an era when the Cold War consensus had come apart, creating policy cross-pressures for hawkish Democrats and dovish Republicans. Cultural values showed a lesser version of the same effect, and if this new voting impact lagged those of both social welfare and national security, its appearance was to be the harbinger of a greatly increased role for the modern period. Lastly, civil rights, clearly aligned by party attachment for this second period, produced a clear if trailing ability to cause rights conservatives among Democrats or rights liberals among Republicans to drift away from their chosen parties.

Yet it would be the modern era that surfaced the greatest change from the original picture (Era 3). Social welfare continued to produce the leading policy stress on party attachments, with an impact greater than in the first or the second postwar eras. Yet social welfare was joined—and implicitly challenged—by cultural values. On the one hand, cultural policy had finally come into a common partisan alignment, though it still lagged those in all three other domains. On the other hand, that meant that culture was now obviously strong enough *and autonomous enough* to challenge social welfare rather than be dominated by it. So an era of cross-cutting pressures from social welfare and cultural values had apparently been born. National security retained some electoral clout, though at a substantial distance—foreign affairs did not disappear from the public mind—while civil rights lagged not just the other three domains in this modern period but its own influence in the preceding era.

Those were composite pictures of policy impact on the presidential vote across three postwar periods. Yet because their focus is policy cross-pressures in the electorate as a whole, it was always possible, and actually quite common, for policy domains to show differential impacts when stratified by party. In other words, Democrats and Republicans could show different relationships to what were otherwise the same policy domains. Moreover, these differential impacts had the potential to vary further at different points in time. At every time, impacts specific to particular parties still had to sum to the national picture. What they did not have to do was be equally influential inside both, a potentially distinguishing feature that was evident from the very first postwar years.

The overall pattern for the electorate as a whole—a major impact from social welfare, little or no impact from anything else—proved to be the same inside both parties. So neither contravened the dominance of social welfare as a voting influence in the opening postwar period (Figure A.2.A and B, Era 1). Yet from an interparty perspective, comparing the two parties with each other, this welfare impact was more than twice as great among Democrats. There were some Republican defections among those whose welfare preferences were more liberal than the bulk of their partisan colleagues. But a one-point movement in the conservative direction on social welfare for a Democrat increased their probability of defecting by about 0.125, while a corresponding move toward liberalism among Republicans had only about half that impact.

Some of this difference must have been more or less mechanical. The opening postwar years were, after all, the period when Democrats had their greatest margin over Republicans in the total electorate. In a socially diverse nation, the party with a substantial majority was likely to encompass a greater diversity of policy preferences. Yet the Democratic Party had simultaneously been the driving force—the vehicle—for a move away from an old politics built around geographic region and toward a new politics built around social class. So as the party driving change, the Democrats were also likely to have the largest share of nominal adherents who had been swept along and found themselves out of sync with a new overall partisan alignment.

The successor era brought greater complexity to policy cross-pressures in the electorate as a whole, and this complexity was once again reflected differentially inside the individual parties (Figure A.2.A and B, Era 2). Welfare preferences remained the leading influence on voter dissidence inside both, while their impact continued to be larger among Democrats than Republicans, even in a period when the share of Republican identifiers was increasing. So a "shaking out" of loyalties that were misaligned in the post–New Deal period still had a great deal farther to go. On the other hand, if this second period was distinguished by the rise of cross-pressures in substantive domains other than social welfare, these fresh voter impacts would also be differentiated not just by party attachment but also by substantive domain.

The four domains were unified by having a greater impact among Democrats than Republicans. The former remained more cross-pressured than the latter. Yet as part of the growing complexity of policy cross-pressures in such a world, each domain went on to feature internal party results peculiar to its own substance, differing not just between the parties but also from one domain to another. Civil rights achieved an augmented influence inside the Democratic Party but was effectively irrelevant to its Republican opposition. Cultural values at least showed

Marginal Effects by Party

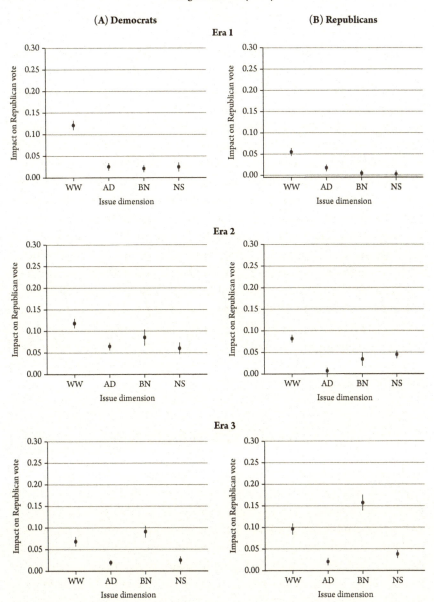

Figure A.2 Marginal Effects by Party

On the x-axis, WW stands for the domain of social welfare, AD for civil rights, BN for cultural values, and NS for national security.

up as a policy stressor among Republicans, but it was more than twice as influential among Democrats. And national security showed the largest of these three secondary impacts among Republicans, though even this was greater in absolute terms among Democrats.

For the modern era, the two parties returned to sharing the same rank-ordering of policy influences (Figure A.2.A and B, Era 3). Yet while social welfare remained the leading influence on voter dissidence when examined for the electorate as a whole, cultural values actually displaced it when examined through the parties individually. In that sense, cultural issues could apply comparatively greater stress to politicking inside the two parties than to the contest between them. So the abstract argument that one or another policy domain might in principle show one impact when all voters were in the analysis but a different impact—even two different impacts—when examined by party reached its ultimate realization with cultural values in the modern era.

That said, the *two* leading domains, social welfare and cultural values, were not just close to parity as voting influences in the nation as a whole but retained that joint dominance when stratified by party, though both were now more influential among Republicans than among Democrats. The strength of policy cross-pressures was greater inside the Republican rather than the Democratic Party for the first time since the end of the Second World War. Yet even that was not quite the end of the story. National security followed cultural values and social welfare at a substantial distance as a source of policy cross-pressures, with civil rights bringing up the rear. Yet national security too was a stronger stressor among Republicans than Democrats, even though it was not very influential in either party. Only civil rights had so little impact that it did not really distinguish the parties at all.

Marginal Effects for the Regions

In the opening years of the postwar period, the great implicit challenge to the organizing power of party attachment came from geographic region. The challenge varied by policy domain, being smallest for social welfare and largest for civil rights. And it varied within domains across time, declining the most on civil rights and surviving the longest on cultural values. All of this more or less requires a look at the potential shaping influence of region on dissident presidential voting. So Figure A.3 returns to comparative marginal effects by policy domain in the total electorate, this time treating the North and the South separately. Figure A.4 will then go on to the story of competing parties within these regions.

For the electorate as a whole in the opening postwar period, welfare preferences were a major source of electoral cross-pressure, and that influence was mirrored strongly in both the North and the South with no real difference between regions (Era 1 in Figure A.3). Yet welfare preferences (WW) were also more or less the total story for voting influences within the national electorate,

Marginal Effects by Region

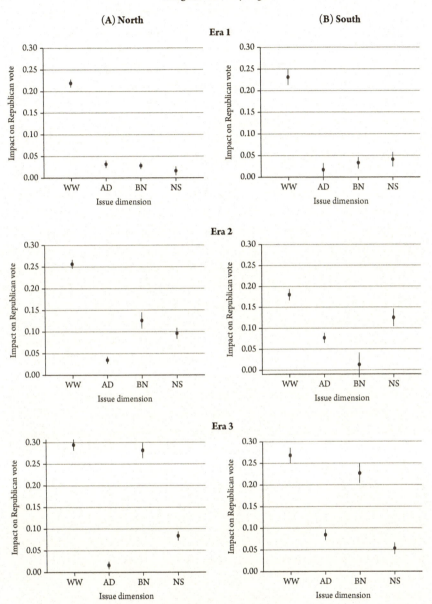

On the X-axis, WW stands for the domain of social welfare, AD for civil rights, BN for cultural values, and NS for national security

Figure A.3 Marginal Effects by Region

On the x-axis, WW stands for the domain of social welfare, AD for civil rights, BN for cultural values, and NS for national security and this too remains accurate when the nation is cut into regional pieces. Finally, the three domains that had nearly no voting influence nationwide, namely civil rights (AD), cultural values (BN), and national security (NS), once again featured roughly equal voting influences by region, at a level of near irrelevance. Chapters 1 to 4 have repeatedly confirmed that region could pull composite partisan alignments into different ideological territory. But region did not go on to make those alignments work in an additionally different fashion in their voting influences, at least in this opening period.

That was a picture that changed in the successor era. Social welfare remained the leading policy influence on a presidential vote for the electorate as a whole, followed by national security in a considerably enhanced role, followed by cultural values with a lesser rise, and lagged by civil rights, though even its voting influence ticked up over the opening period. Yet this time, the two regions responded very differently within that national picture, to the point of generating distinct regional patterns of voter dissidence that made a synoptic national portrait look evidently misleading, revealing it to be an amalgam—and in that sense an artifact—of two quite different regional pictures (Era 2 in Figure A.3).

Indeed, this second era, not the opening years and not the modern era, would be the period when the two great regions were most disparate in the comparative standing of their voter influences. In the North, social welfare was far and away the dominant source of policy cross-pressures on party attachment, followed at a distance by an augmented cultural values, followed by a stepped-up national security, with civil rights still largely an irrelevance. In the South, social welfare was likewise the leading domain for partisan stress, though its impact fell well below the Northern counterpart, while every other policy domain assumed a different order, South versus North. Below the Mason-Dixon line, it was national security that jumped up the most, followed by a sharply increased influence for civil rights, while cultural values was the domain showing nearly no voter effect.

The rise of party and the decline of region as organizing principles for partisan alignments in this second postwar period, now for civil rights plus national security and not just social welfare, did increase the potential for partisan stress in domains where party attachment was previously absent. Voters could now know—or at least, it was harder to avoid knowing—whether they were or were not in sync with their chosen party in a range of policy realms, a possibility that caused more turmoil among voters in the South than in the North on national security, and much more on civil rights. Only cultural values still lacked a systematic linkage to party attachment at this point, and that allowed cultural issues to show an augmented voting influence in the more culturally diverse North but not in the more culturally homogeneous South.

The modern world was to experience a growing convergence across partisan alignments, and this had to constrict regional diversity. As it developed, the major voting influences, from social welfare and cultural values, were slightly more influential in the North than in the South, but the difference was small compared to their shared distance from the voting impacts of national security and civil rights (Era 3 in Figure A.3). That left the two great political regions with distinguishable voting influences only in the less influential policy domains, national security and especially civil rights. Between the two, national security was more influential in the North, while civil rights was much more influential in the South.

So if substantive diversity and regional divergence had been the twin themes of the second postwar period when subjected to a voting analysis, a further reshuffling of voter influences came to characterize the modern era, with two hugely influential policy domains that showed only minor differences by region, along with two domains that retained regional differences, but only on a less consequential level. Across all three eras, social welfare continued to stand out as the most uniform voting influence, now across both major regions as well. By contrast, cultural values was the most volatile, breaking through in the North but not in the South in the second postwar period before peaking in both for the modern era. Once it moved onto the policy dial, civil rights was consistently more influential in the South than in the North. And national security showed a temporal rather than a regional pattern, rising in the middle period for both regions before declining again for both in the modern era.

What remains in a search for the marginal effects of four policy domains by region is to ask whether the individual parties *inside* the two major regions were doing things that were sufficiently different as to alter not just the regional story but also its contribution to a national picture. Such comparisons risk becoming overly fine-grained, quickly outrunning the ability of the data to provide reliable results for what can be a numerically small body of dissidents when stratified both by party and by region in a given policy domain. Still, it should be possible to say for each of the three postwar periods whether individual parties within specific regions were doing something strongly dissident from an overall picture by party or by region.[1] To that end, Figure A.4 takes the regional stories from Figure A.3 and carves them one more time, by parties within regions.

In the immediate postwar years, the only policy domain with a consequential effect on presidential voting for the nation as a whole had been social welfare. Stratification by region had contributed nothing further, producing what were close to identical portraits, North versus South. Adding party to the national picture had shown that the impact of welfare preferences was considerably larger among Democrats than among Republicans. Now, broken out one more time by parties within regions, there is one small further twist: the Southern Democrats were showing by far the most internal upheaval in this first postwar period. They were clearly the most stressed by social welfare, while

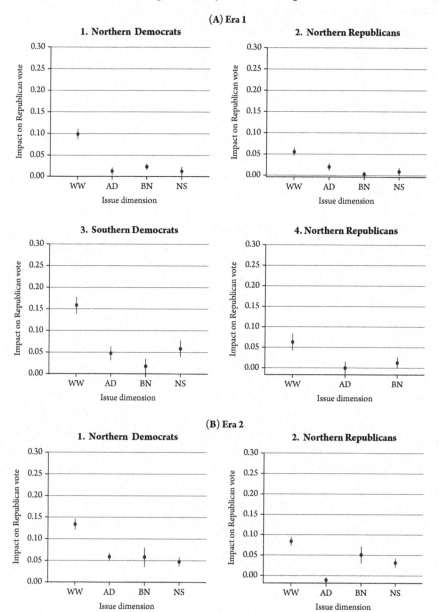

Figure A.4 Marginal Effects by Parties within Regions

On the x-axis, WW stands for the domain of social welfare, AD for civil rights, BN for cultural values, and NS for national security.

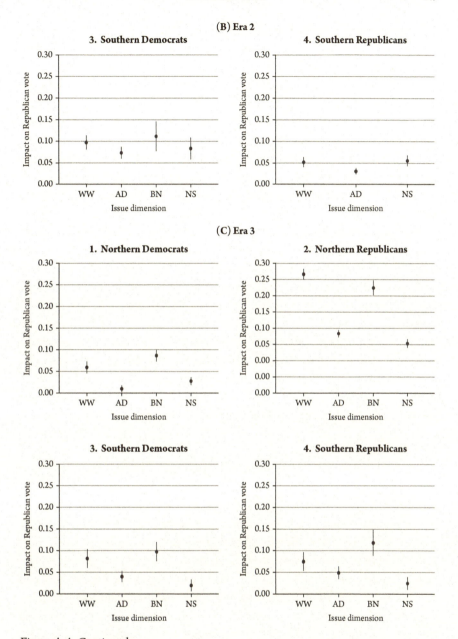

Figure A.4 Continued

civil rights and national security, while far less troubled within any of the four regional parties, were of any consequence only among Southern Democrats (Figure A.4.A.1, 2, 3, and 4).

In the successor period, social welfare continued to be the leading influence on voter defection nationally, but all three other domains came to life on a secondary level. Stratified by region, social welfare and cultural values were more influential in the North—this was actually a harbinger of the national picture to come—while civil rights and national security were more influential in the South. Broken out additionally by parties within regions, Democratic Parties suffered greater electoral stress than Republican Parties in both, though the source of this stress varied itself by region (Figure A.4.B.1, 2, 3, and 4). Northern Democrats were more stressed than Southern Democrats by social welfare, while Southern Democrats were more stressed in the three other domains than were their Northern brethren. Overall, Southern Democrats were most clearly in turmoil, being stressed by all four major policy domains and to roughly the same degree.

The single most consequential story of electoral impact in the modern era was then to be the explosive rise of cultural values as a voting influence—in the nation, in the two parties, in the two regions, and now in the four regionalized parties as well (Figure A.4.C.1, 2, 3, and 4). Social welfare and cultural values became jointly the serious voting influences, while civil rights and national security lagged well behind. Yet where electoral turmoil had been most intense among Southern Democrats in the two preceding eras, it became most intense among Northern Republicans in the modern era. Culture was more divisive among these Northern Republicans than anywhere else, but if their division on social welfare was smaller than this cultural division, even it was likewise the largest among the four regional parties.

Last Word

Much else could be observed through systematic displays of voting impact by policy domain. Thus, similar displays could be provided for any alternative cleavage, at least any that offered sufficient numbers to permit the analysis. Such displays could likewise be provided for any *combination* of cleavages: low-income Evangelical female Democrats, middle-income Catholic male Republicans, and on and on. Many of these run quickly into the problem of insufficient samples, even for the nation as a whole, even for the cohort as a whole. But almost all run into the problem that social backgrounds, policy preferences, and party attachments are already instantiated in partisan alignments before any given vote occurs, risking very unreliable conclusions when the focus is the small minority of party defectors within such specialized subpopulations.

That is, of course, one last pragmatic rationale for all of the preceding, for a search for the social roots of political conflicts. A look at those who did *not* cast a vote in line with their party attachments and who also possessed discordant preferences in various policy domains, gathered in a small set of intermediary groups, has been our strategy for offering a voting analysis that can contribute something within those constraints. But in the end, the main intellectual task is—and has to be—the prior one, the one involving attention to major social cleavages, to the policy preferences that emerged from those roots, to the transmission of this linkage into party attachments, and ultimately to a set of ever-evolving partisan alignments. That is what has been addressed in Chapters 2 through 4 and the Conclusion, summarized and extended in the afterword. It is, in our view, the evolving structural context of American politics.

Appendix

DATA AND MEASURES

The data and measures that underpin this analysis were originally created for William J. M. Claggett and Byron E. Shafer, *The American Public Mind: The Issue Structure of Postwar Politics in the United States* (Cambridge: Cambridge University Press, 2010). While that book offers multiple substantive arguments, it is also in effect a 280-page introduction to these measures. The dataset was then extended in Byron E. Shafer and Regina L. Wagner, *The Long War over Party Structure: Democratic Representation and Policy Responsiveness in American Politics* (Cambridge: Cambridge University Press, 2019), where it played a very different role, tracking the impacts of structural reform across time.

For both books plus *The Social Roots of American Politics*, a comprehensive set of policy preferences began with a set of hypotheses drawn from postwar political history about the major domains of policy conflict during this extended era. We believed that four major substantive domains were widely taken to characterize this period: social welfare, civil rights, foreign affairs, and cultural values. Creation of four relevant measures then had to meet two essential criteria. First, individual items for each domain had to have *face validity*. That is, the surface content of any such items had to reflect critical elements of the theoretical definition. Second, those individual items had to *scale collectively*. That is, appropriate surface contents had to be correlated, so that they were in fact measuring facets of the same underlying phenomenon.

Issue items that unambiguously referenced welfare, foreign, race, or cultural policy were then subjected to exploratory factor analyses, domain by domain and year by year. Fortunately, consistent measures for each did follow from the relevant substantive definitions. That is, all scaled appropriately in an exploratory factor analysis (EFA). At that point, it was necessary to turn to confirmatory factor analysis (CFA) in order to confront an existing set of hypotheses from the professional literature while commenting on the inductively derived findings

(EFAs) from our own exploratory analysis. In formal terms, CFA applies prior theory and its evidence to specify relationships between one or more latent (unobservable) factors along with a set of observable variables that these factors are hypothesized to affect.

In this way, the observed variables become indicators for those latent factors, and the first substantive realm to produce a consistent measure with political implications was social welfare, the policy domain at the center of the New Deal. The items contributing to a welfare index would vary with the array of relevant questions that were asked in a changing American National Election Study (ANES), yet they could be isolated repeatedly within a single explicit definition of the policy realm:

> *Social welfare* involves efforts to protect citizens against the randomness— that is, the harshness and individual inequities—of the economic marketplace. While there are myriad ways to accomplish this, direct personal benefits are the crucial touchstone, while *social insurance* provides the irreducible programmatic core.

Inside this array, certain "marker" items, widely accepted as belonging to the welfare domain, did recur. So they provided reasonable assurance that a slowly changing measure captured the same basic policy concerns over time. Among these markers for social welfare were:

> Some people feel the government in Washington should see to it that every person has a job and a good standard of living. Others think the government should just let each person get ahead on their own.
>
> Some feel there should be a government insurance plan that would cover all medical and hospital expenses for everyone. Others feel that medical expenses should be paid by individuals, and through private insurance like Blue Cross or other company-paid plans.

Items contributing to the civil rights index likewise varied with the array of substantively relevant questions that were asked in a gradually changing ANES. Yet they too could be isolated to fall within a single explicit definition of the policy realm across time, and refining this was even easier for civil rights than for social welfare:

> *Civil rights* could have been given an abstract formulation, making it a subdomain of civil liberties. Yet civil rights in the postwar period has been most centrally a matter of race policy for black Americans, so in the

search for a recurrent issue structure, it seemed essential to retain *racial concerns* as the essence of a policy definition.

Once more, certain marker items, even more generally accepted as belonging to the rights domain, provided the same sort of assurance that a slowly changing measure captured the same basic policy focus. Among these markers were:

> Some people feel that if black people are not getting fair treatment in jobs, the government in Washington ought to see to it that they do. Others feel that this is not the federal government's business.
>
> Some people say that the government in Washington should see to it that white and black children are allowed to go to the same schools. Others claim that this is not the government's business.

Students of public opinion may have differed more about the basic possibility of such a measure for international relations and foreign affairs, where some believed in a very fickle public. Yet a formal definition of the domain was easy enough to generate:

> *International relations* involves connections between the United States and the non-American world. Foreign policy thus reflects efforts to manage the interaction of the United States—its government, its citizens, and their organizations—with the same elements of other nations.

Approached this way, public preferences in international relations did have a less simple dimensionality than those in any of the other three major realms. Yet prior analyses had highlighted policy issues concerning *national security* as arguably the cluster of opinions most often central to preferences on foreign policy, and the available measure of policy preferences on national security is straightforward and easily recognized. Early marker items were focused on the Cold War, itself impressively long-running, while later markers were focused on defense preparedness. Yet all correlated and all aligned. Fortunately, the key marker entered the ANES before the Cold War ended, so that correlation and alignment with earlier items can be guaranteed:

> Some people believe that we should spend much less money for defense. Others feel that defense spending should be greatly increased.

The final major (but growing) realm of postwar policy conflict that was widely recognized in the professional literature was cultural values. As the newest of the four, it did elicit the broadest array of items intended to tap public preferences, yet it was easy to offer an abstract definition, potentially capable of isolating items with a common latent content, a definition centered on *behavioral norms*:

> *Cultural values* involves the norms within which social life should proceed, and cultural policy involves the governmental role in supporting those norms. The flashpoints for conflict over cultural policy in the postwar period were heterogeneous in the extreme; that is the great challenge of the realm. Yet *the character of social life* is in some sense the focus of them all.

Fortunately, a set of marker items from the available array did recur sufficiently to underpin a measure with appropriate substantive foci, including the public role of religion, abortion policy, sex roles, and homosexual rights.

> Some people think it is all right for the public schools to start each day with a prayer. Others feel that religion does not belong in the public schools but should be taken care of by the family and the church.
>
> Abortion should never be permitted; abortion should be permitted only if the life and health of the woman is in danger; abortion should be permitted if, due to personal reasons, the woman would have difficulty in caring for the child; abortion should never be forbidden, since one should not require a woman to have a child she does not want.
>
> Some people feel that women should have an equal role with men in running business, industry, and government. Other people feel that women's place is in the home.
>
> Do you favor or oppose laws to protect homosexuals against job discrimination?

Those are the critical products from an EFA of ANES items with potential relevance to four major policy domains. Table App.1 offers two such examples, to suggest the range of final results from subjecting those measures to CFA. For this, version 7.0 of AMOS was used, offering full-information maximum likelihood estimation in the presence of missing data, a superior way of handling

APPENDIX

Table A.1 Exploratory Factor Analyses

A. Social Welfare, 1984

Variable Description	Factor Loading	Communality
Social Security	0.72	0.51
Medicare	0.72	0.51
Food Stamps	0.70	0.49
Unemployment	0.68	0.46
Guaranteed Job	0.66	0.43
Public Schools	0.58	0.33
Health Insurance	0.49	0.24
Eigenvalue	2.98	$N = 669$

B. Cultural Values, 1992

Variable Description	Factor Loading	Communality
Abortion Policy Index	0.78	0.60
Gay Rights Index	0.73	0.60
Women's Roles Index	0.68	0.47
School Prayer	0.40	0.16
Eigenvalue	2.04	$N = 1,030$

that problem in the confirmatory analysis. This comes with a full statistical interpretation of the models being tested, along with a graphic display of their relationships.

The ANES of 1992 is particularly good at showing the power and reach of these analyses, since this was a year in which the ANES paid particular attention to attitudinal structure, through an especially rich array of policy items. Figure App.1 shows the structure of welfare preferences in 1992. In this year, the continuing subdimension of *structural welfare*, the classic marker for the entire domain, managed to gather and organize thirteen substantive items. Figure App.2 then shows the structure of cultural preferences in that same year. Most important here is that in this data-rich year, the subdimension of *behavioral norms*, again the classic marker for the entire domain, features all four of its defining components, with four items on abortion policy, two on gay rights, two on women's roles, plus the ongoing item on school prayer.

APPENDIX

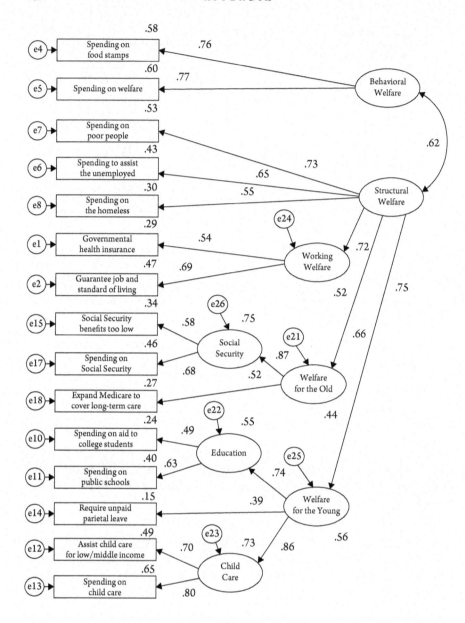

Standardized estimates
Chi-Square = 397.011; df = 83; p = .000

Figure A.1 Confirmatory Factor Analysis of Social Welfare Items, 1992

APPENDIX 159

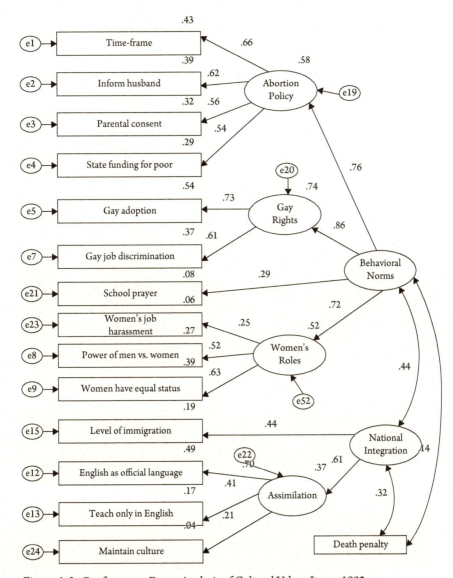

Figure A.2 Confirmatory Factor Analysis of Cultural Values Items, 1992

NOTES

Introduction

1. An earlier effort to pursue political implications from the same four cleavages is Jeff Manza and Clem Brooks, *Social Cleavages and Political Change: Voter Alignments and U.S. Party Coalitions* (New York: Oxford University Press, 1999). A landmark predecessor is Seymour Martin Lipset, *Political Man: The Social Bases of Politics* (Garden City, NY: Doubleday, 1960).
2. Among many, see Alonzo L. Hamby, *The Imperial Years: The United States since 1939* (London: Weybright and Talley, 1976); James T. Patterson, *Grand Expectations: The United States, 1945–1974* (New York: Oxford University Press, 1996); Michael Barone, *Our Country: The Shaping of America from Roosevelt to Reagan* (New York: Free Press, 1990).
3. This is the standard two-part question, asking for a party identification first, then either for the strength of that identification or for a regular partisan leaning among those who deny an initial identification. For the canonical use, see "The Impact of Party Identification," Chapter 5, in Angus Campbell, Philip E. Converse, Warren E. Miller, and Donald E. Stokes, *The American Voter*, abr. ed. (New York: John Wiley, 1964). For subsequent reflections, Warren E. Miller and J. Merrill Shanks, "Conceptualization and Measurement of Party Identification," in *The New American Voter* (Cambridge, MA: Harvard University Press, 1996), Chapter 6.
4. A comprehensive introduction to the data and to measures of policy preference in the four domains used here is William J. M. Claggett and Byron E. Shafer, *The American Public Mind: The Issue Structure of Mass Politics in the Postwar United States* (New York: Cambridge University Press, 2010). For their utilization in a very different context, see Byron E. Shafer and Regina L. Wagner, *The Long War over Party Structure: Democratic Representation and Policy Responsiveness in American Politics* (Cambridge: Cambridge University Press, 2019).
5. The literature bearing on regional politics at various points in American history is voluminous. Yet the resurgence of regional cleavages at an early point within battles over the welfare state somehow came as a surprise (and disappointment) to many analysts. James T. Patterson, *Congressional Conservatism and the New Deal* (Lexington: University Press of Kentucky, 1967); Ira Katznelson, *Fear Itself: The New Deal and the Origins of Our Time* (New York: Norton, 2013).
6. In William J. M. Claggett and Philip H. Pollock III, "The Modes of Participation Revisited, 1980–2004," *Political Research Quarterly* 59(2006), 593–600, the authors concluded that the diagnostic behaviors for political activism were campaign participation and financial contribution, and we have used this focus in our own measure of activism.

Chapter 1

1. For the runup to postwar welfare conflict, see David M. Kennedy, *Freedom from Fear, the American People in Depression and War* (New York: Oxford University Press, 1999), and Michael Barone, *Our Country: The Shaping of America from Roosevelt to Reagan* (New York: Free Press, 1990), especially Parts I and II, "Our Country 1930" and "Turmoil."

2. For a systematic overview of the various positions, see "The Sociological Tradition in Political Behavior Research," Chapter 1 in Jeff Manza and Clem Brooks, *Social Cleavages and Political Change: Voter Alignments and U.S. Policy Coalitions* (Oxford: Oxford University Press, 1999). For a wide-ranging taste of associated arguments about social class, see Terry Nichols and Seymour Martin Lipset, eds., *The Breakdown of Class Politics: A Debate on Post-Industrial Stratification* (Washington, DC: Woodrow Wilson Center Press, 2001).

3. On the creation of the ANES, see Warren E. Miller, "An Organizational History of the Institutional Origins of the National Election Studies," *European Journal of Political Research* 25(1994), 247–265. For the story in the longer run, see Jean M. Converse, *Survey Research in the United States: Roots and Emergence, 1890–1960* (Berkeley: University of California Press, 1987).

4. Herbert McClosky, Paul Hoffman, and Rosemary O'Hara, "Issue Conflict and Consensus among Party Leaders and Followers," *American Political Science Review* 54(1960), 406–472. For a focus on social welfare as a policy domain, see Edwin Amenta, *Bold Relief: Institutional Politics and the Origins of Modern American Social Policy* (Princeton, NJ: Princeton University Press, 1998), and Edward D. Berkowitz, *America's Welfare State: From Roosevelt to Reagan* (Baltimore: Johns Hopkins University, 1991).

5. An overview with substantial attention to social welfare and party attachment is Everett Carll Ladd Jr., with Charles D. Hadley, *Transformations of the American Party System: Political Coalitions from the New Deal to the 1970s* (New York: W. W. Norton, 1975), especially Chapters 1 and 2, "The Formation of the New Deal Party System" and "The Extension of the New Deal Party System." For a focus on the Republicans, Robert Mason, *The Republican Party in American Politics from Hoover to Reagan* (Cambridge: Cambridge University Press, 2012), especially Chapters 1–4.

6. See John Lewis Gaddis, *The United States and the Origins of the Cold War, 1941–1947* (New York: Columbia University Press, 1972), and Alonzo L. Hamby, *The Imperial Years: The United States since 1939* (New York: Weybright and Talley, 1976).

7. For isolationism, see Wayne S. Cole, *Roosevelt and the Isolationists, 1932–1945* (Lincoln: University of Nebraska Press, 1982), and Justus D. Doenecke, *Not to the Swift: The Old Isolationists in the Cold War Era* (Lewisburg, PA: Bucknell University Press, 1979). For the general public and the coming of the Cold War, see James T. Patterson, *Grand Expectations: The United States, 1945–1974* (New York: Oxford University Press, 1996), especially Chapter 4, "Grand Expectations about the World," and Chapter 5, "Hardening of the Cold War, 1945–1948."

8. For our approach to applying this distinction, see note 6 in the Preface.

9. For a variety of approaches to what he calls "the democratic class struggle" of the time, see Seymour Martin Lipset, *Political Man: The Social Bases of Politics* (New York: Doubleday, 1960), most especially Chapters 7 and 8, "Elections: The Expression of the Democratic Class Struggle" and "Elections: The Expression of the Democratic Class Struggle—Continuity and Change."

10. Moreover, as we shall see in the next section of this chapter, this internal Democratic alignment was being restrained for the nation as a whole by the ideological dissidence of Southern Democratic activists.

11. For regions abstractly, see Michael Bradshaw, *Regions and Regionalism in the United States* (Jackson: University of Mississippi Press, 1988). For a regional approach to American politics using a different cut from the simple North/South divide, see Richard F. Bensel, *Sectionalism and American Political Development, 1880–1980* (Madison: University of Wisconsin Press, 1984).

12. An introduction to this way of thinking is Giovanni Sartori, *Parties and Party System: A Framework for Analysis* (New York: Cambridge University Press, 1976). For systems with two major parties, see Alan Ware, *The Dynamics of Two-Party Politics: Party Structures and the Management of Competition* (London: Oxford University Press, 2009).

13. The vast bulk of work on regional politics in the United States since the Second World War has focused on the South as the dissident region. One deliberate effort to do the same kind of analysis outside the South in the postwar world is Howard L. Reiter and Jeffrey M. Stonecash, *Counter Realignment: Political Change in the Northeastern United States* (Cambridge: Cambridge University Press, 2011).

NOTES

14. The classic summary of Southern politics at the opening of the postwar period was V. O. Key Jr., *Southern Politics in State and Nation* (New York: Knopf, 1947). It was preceded by W. J. Cash, *The Mind of the South* (New York: Knopf, 1941) as a general introduction to Southern culture.

15. An early postwar overview is Louis M. Seagull, *Southern Republicanism* (Cambridge, MA: Schenkman, 1975). An important predecessor is Alexander Heard, *A Two-Party South?* (Chapel Hill: University of North Carolina Press, 1952).

16. Both are richly explored in Devin Caughey, *The Unsolid South: Mass Politics and National Representation in a One-Party Enclave* (Princeton, NJ: Princeton University Press, 2018).

17. Their situation at the time is systematically explored in Everett Carll Ladd Jr., *Negro Political Leadership in the South* (New York: Atheneum, 1969).

18. Caughey, *The Unsolid South,* pays serious attention to economic policy, the general public, and the wealthy within it, especially in Chapter 4, "Southern Democrats in Congress."

19. This idiosyncratic—nonlinear—story could be rolled on and on. Thus, if upper-class Southern Democrats "should" have been Republican courtesy of their welfare preferences, then middle-income Republicans "should" have been Democratic by the same standard.

20. Overviews of American politics during these successor periods would include Iwan W. Morgan, *Beyond the Liberal Consensus: A Political History of the United States since 1965* (London: Hurst, 1994); Edward D. Berkowitz, *Something Happened: A Political and Cultural Overview of the Seventies* (New York: Columbia University Press, 2006); John Ehrman, *The Eighties: America in the Age of Reagan* (New Haven, CT: Yale University Press, 2005); James T. Patterson, *Restless Giant: The United States from Watergate to Bush v. Gore* (New York: Oxford University Press, 2005).

21. Among others, see Robert X. Browning, *Politics and Social Welfare Policy in the United States* (Knoxville: University of Tennessee Press, 1986); Edward D. Berkowitz, *America's Welfare State: From Roosevelt to Reagan* (Baltimore: Johns Hopkins University Press, 1991); and James T. Patterson, *America's Struggle against Poverty, 1900–1994* (Cambridge, MA: Harvard University Press, 1994).

22. A view of the evolution of social class in American politics, drawing important further distinctions within the general category, is "Class," Chapter 3 in Manza and Brooks, *Social Cleavages and Political Change.*

23. This has been an important focus in the literature on political change in the South, though often presented within a national framework. See John R. Petrocik, "Realignment: New Party Coalitions and the Nationalization of the South," *Journal of Politics* 49(1987), 347–375, and Harold W. Stanley, "Southern Partisan Changes: Dealignment, Realignment, or Both?," *Journal of Politics* 50(1988), 65–88.

24. The travails of the Republican Party in finding a policy position that could satisfy the active party while attracting an electoral majority are central to Robert Mason, *The Republican Party in American Politics from Hoover to Reagan* (Cambridge: Cambridge University Press, 2012), and well covered additionally in Barone, *Our Country,* especially Part 3, "Confidence," Chapters 21–37.

25. For another example of contrary moves by activists and their (putative) rank and file, from the other party and in a different policy domain, see Edward G. Carmines and James A. Stimson, *Issues Evolution: Race and the Transformation of American Politics* (Princeton, NJ: Princeton University Press, 1989), especially Chapter 4, "Political Activism and the Party System."

26. For more on Southern political evolution, see David Lublin, *The Republican South: Democratization and Partisan Change* (Princeton, NJ: Princeton University Press, 2004), and Byron E. Shafer and Richard Johnston, *The End of Southern Exceptionalism? Class, Race, and Partisan Change in the Postwar South* (Cambridge, MA: Harvard University Press, 2006).

27. A treatment of this Republican story as a kind of mirror image of Southern Democratic evolution is Reiter and Stonecash, *Counter Realignment.*

28. For the changing economic structure of the South as a region, see James C. Cobb, *Industrialization and Southern Society, 1877–1984* (Lexington: University of Kentucky Press, 1984); Philip Scranton, ed., *The Second Wave; Southern Industrialization from the 1940s to the 1970s* (Athens: University of Georgia Press, 2001); and Bernard L. Weinstein, *Regional Growth and Decline in the United States,* 2nd ed. (New York: Praeger, 1985).

NOTES

29. For a dissection of this development from a perspective much closer to it in time, see Ladd with Hadley, *Transformations of American Politics*, Chapter 3, "First Rendings: The Case of the South."

30. A party in such parlous condition in the immediate postwar years, and for so long beforehand, was perhaps inevitably relegated to a side note in most treatments of the Southern politics of the time. But helpful background begins once again with Key, *Southern Politics*, Chapter 13, "A Note on the Republican Party." A condensed but fuller background opens Nicol C. Rae, *Southern Democrats* (New York: Oxford University Press, 1994), especially Chapter 1, "The South and American Party Factionalism," and Chapter 2, "The Old Southern Democracy and Its Erosion, 1876 to 1965."

31. Note additionally that while lower-class Southern Democrats now looked impressively liberal, they had moved no farther between periods than these upper-class counterparts. This lower-class shift in Table 1.11.C was from −.19 to −.39, a net of .20. The same shift among high-income Democrats in the South was from +.14 to −.07, a net of .21. And the same shift among middle-income Republicans, still in the South, was −.01 to +.24, for a net of .25— clearly the largest such move from the first to the second eras.

32. See note 9 earlier. Having begun with a high but essentially uniform support for the Democratic Party in all three classes, the South inevitably offered more scope for an impact from, for an impact over time, Lipset's "democratic class struggle."

33. Among many, see Otis L. Graham Jr., *The Great Campaigns: Reform and War in America, 1900–1928* (Englewood Cliffs, NJ: Prentice-Hall, 1971); Michael McGerr, *A Fierce Discontent: The Rise and Fall of the Progressive Movement in America, 1870–1920* (New York: Oxford University Press, 2005); and Ellis W. Hawley, *The Great War and the Search for a Modern Order* (Prospect Heights, IL: Waveland Press, 1997).

34. For the argument that this was an evolving process rather than a clean break, see especially Helmut Norpoth, Andrew H. Sidman, and Clara H. Suong, "Polls and Elections: The New Deal Realignment in Real Time," *Presidential Studies Quarterly* 43(2013), 146–166. See also Eric Schickler and Devin Caughey, "Public Opinion, Organized Labor, and the Limits of New Deal Liberalism, 1936–1945," *Studies in American Political Development* 25(2011), 162–189.

35. A vigorous dissent from various arguments about the diminution of social welfare and the decline of social class is Geoffrey Evans and James Tilley in their study of the same concerns inside British politics, where the penultimate chapter says, "Class Politics Is Dead," and the final chapter asserts instead, "Long Live Class Politics." Evans and Tilley, *The New Politics of Class: The Political Exclusion of the British Working Class* (Oxford: Oxford University Press, 2017).

36. For the active party, see Mason, *The Republican Party and American Politics from Hoover to Reagan*. See also David W. Reinhardt, *The Republican Right since 1945* (Lexington: University Press of Kentucky, 1983).

37. Besides Rae, *Southern Democrats*, see Stanley P. Berard, *Southern Democrats in the U.S. House of Representatives* (Norman: University of Oklahoma Press, 2001).

38. See Byron E. Shafer, *The American Political Pattern: Stability and Change, 1932–2016* (Lawrence: University Press of Kansas, 2016), especially Chapter 2, "The Long Arm of the New Deal: The Political Structure of the Late New Deal Era, 1969–1992."

Chapter 2

1. Particularly helpful are Richard M. Valelly, *The Two Reconstructions: The Struggle for Black Enfranchisement* (Chicago: University of Chicago Press, 2004), and Hugh Davis Graham, *The Civil Rights Era: Origins and Development of National Policy, 1960–1972* (New York: Oxford University Press, 1990).

2. As with Article I of the Constitution of the United States; Martha S. Jones, *Birthright Citizens: A History of Race and Rights in Antebellum America* (Cambridge: Cambridge University Press, 2018; Eric Foner, *The Second Founding: How the Civil War and Reconstruction Remade the Constitution* (New York: W. W. Norton, 2019); Williamjames H. Hoffer, *Plessy v. Ferguson: Race and Inequality in Jim Crow America* (Lawrence: University Press of Kansas, 2018).

NOTES

3. For the years before there was an ANES, central texts are C. Vann Woodward, *The Strange Career of Jim Crow* (New York: Oxford University Press, 1955), and V. O. Key Jr., *Southern Politics in State and Nation* (New York: Knopf, 1949).

4. For two systematic examinations of the relationship between social class and racial background among black Americans, see Michael C. Dawson, *Behind the Mule: Race and Class in African American Politics* (Princeton, NJ: Princeton University Press, 1995), and William Julius Wilson, *The Declining Significance of Race* (Chicago: University of Chicago Press, 1981). For consideration of their strategic implications, see Wilson, *The Bridge over the Racial Divide: Rising Inequality and Coalition Politics* (Berkeley: University of California Press, 1999).

5. A perception that the historical narrative would certainly support, as with William E. Leuchtenburg, *Franklin D. Roosevelt and the New Deal, 1932–1940* (New York: Harper & Row, 1963), and Anthony J. Badger, *The New Deal: The Depression Years* (Chicago: Ivan R. Dee, 1989).

6. For the Republican Party and civil rights, see William E. Gienapp, *The Origins of the Republican Party, 1852–1856* (New York: Oxford University Press, 1987), and Lewis L. Gould, *The Republicans: A History of the Grand Old Party* (New York: Random House, 2003). For the Republican resistance to the welfare state, see Robert Mason, *The Republican Party and American Politics from Hoover to Reagan* (Cambridge: Cambridge University Press, 2012), Chapters 1–4; see also Joseph Boskin, *Opposition Politics: The Anti-New Deal Tradition* (Beverly Hills, CA: Glencoe, 1968).

7. The metaphor itself does additional work in Byron E. Shafer and Richard Johnston, *The End of Southern Exceptionalism: Class, Race, and Partisan Change in the Postwar South* (Cambridge, MA: Harvard University Press, 2006).

8. Jeff Manza and Clem Brooks delve even more broadly into this divide in "Race and the Social Bases of Voter Alignments," Chapter 6, in Manza and Brooks, *Social Cleavages and Political Change: Voter Alignments and U.S. Party Coalitions* (Oxford: Oxford University Press, 1999). They find the strongest cleavage for isolating extreme voting behavior to be race, though this racial divide does little to reduce the power of the class cleavage.

9. This presumption was articulated explicitly in Key, *Southern Politics in State and Nation*, and shared by Alexander Heard, *A Two-Party South?* (Chapel Hill: University of North Carolina Press, 1952). It would give rise to—and be largely shared by—a voluminous subsequent literature on Southern politics.

10. The two pieces of legislation are centerpieces in Graham, *The Civil Rights Era*. For earlier efforts, see Jeffrey A. Jenkins and Justin Peck, "Building toward Major Policy Change: Congressional Action on Civil Rights, 1941–1950," *Law and History Review* 31(2013), 139–189. For judicial contributions to the same cause, see Michael J. Klarman, *From Jim Crow to Civil Rights: The Supreme Court in the Struggle for Racial Equality* (New York: Oxford University Press, 2004).

11. On the amendment itself, see Elaine Weiss, *The Woman's Hour: The Great Fight to Win the Vote* (New York: Viking, 2018); on its impact, see Christina Wolbrecht and J. Kevin Corder, *A Century of Votes for Women: American Elections Since Suffrage* (Cambridge: Cambridge University Press, 2020).

12. For the central black increment, see Katherine Tate, *From Protest to Politics: The New American Black Voters* (Cambridge, MA: Harvard University Press, 1993). For broader spillover effects from the struggle for enfranchisement, see James W. Button, *Blacks and Social Change: Impact of the Civil Rights Movement in Southern Communities* (Princeton, NJ: Princeton University Press, 1989).

13. Especially focused and helpful is Eric Schickler, *Racial Realignment: The Transformation of American Liberalism, 1932–1965* (Princeton, NJ: Princeton University Press, 2016), and Everett Carll Ladd Jr., with Charles D. Hadley, "Intertwining," Part I in Ladd with Hadley, *Transformations of the American Party System* (New York: W. W. Norton, 1978).

14. For the truly grand context for these developments, see Ira Berlin, *The Making of African America: The Four Great Migrations* (New York: Viking, 2010). For a rich picture of the South-to-North migration within that framework, see Nicholas Lemann, *The Promised Land: The Great Black Migration and How It Changed America* (New York: Random House, 1991).

NOTES

15. For black politics in the North before reform, see James Q. Wilson, *Negro Politics: The Search for Leadership* (New York: Free Press, 1960); for black politics in the South before reform, see Everett Carll Ladd Jr., *Negro Political Leadership in the South* (New York: Atheneum, 1969).

16. A residuum of black Republicanism, never evident in the North, could still be glimpsed in Southern survey data, though it was always small and constantly declining.

17. This is not to say that a civil rights politics somehow missed the Northern region, as with James R. Ralph Jr., *Northern Protest: Martin Luther King, Jr., Chicago, and the Civil Rights Movement* (Cambridge, MA: Harvard University Press, 1993).

18. For the beginnings of this Republican evolution, see Louis M. Seagull, *Southern Republicanism* (Cambridge, MA: Schenkman, 1975); Numan V. Bartley and Hugh D. Graham, *Southern Politics and the Second Reconstruction* (Baltimore: Johns Hopkins University Press, 1975).

19. Alexander P. Lamis, *The Two-Party South* (New York: Oxford University Press, 1984); Earl Black and Merle Black, *The Rise of Southern Republicans* (Cambridge, MA: Harvard University Press, 2002).

20. This is not so say that they had not reached this point through a nearly hundred-year odyssey of their own: Alan Ware, *The Democratic Party Heads North, 1877–1962* (Cambridge: Cambridge University Press, 2006).

21. The struggles of Southern Democratic elected officials to cope with this changing context are captured in Nicol C. Rae, *The Southern Democrats* (New York: Oxford University Press, 1994), and Stanley P. Berard, *Southern Democrats in the U.S. House of Representatives* (Norman: University of Oklahoma Press, 2001). For the roots of those struggles, see Devin Caughey, *The Unsolid South: Mass Politics and National Representation in a One-Party Enclave* (Princeton, NJ: Princeton University Press, 2018).

Chapter 3

1. An intellectual forefather of this way of thinking is Seymour Martin Lipset and Stein Rokkan, "Cleavage Structures, Party Systems, and Voter Alignments," the Introduction to Lipset and Rokkan, eds., *Party Systems and Voter Alignments: Cross-National Perspectives* (New York: Free Press, 1967). Subsequent products in the same tradition would include Byron E. Shafer and William J. M. Claggett, *The Two Majorities: The Issue Context of Modern American Politics* (Baltimore: Johns Hopkins University Press, 1995), and Mark D. Brewer and Jeffrey M. Stonecash, *Split: Class and Cultural Divides in American Politics* (Washington, DC: CQ Press, 2006).

2. The rich range of possibilities by which this religious seedbed could produce political fruit are surveyed in Jeff Manza and Clem Brooks, "What Is the Religious Cleavage?," in Manza and Brooks, *Social Cleavages and Political Change: Voter Alignments and U.S. Party Coalitions* (Oxford: Oxford University Press, 1999), 89–91. For thinking about the process by which this occurs, see Ted Jelen, *The Political Mobilization of Religious Beliefs* (New York: Praeger, 1991).

3. Four very different routes into that perception were David Riesman, *The Lonely Crowd: A Study of the Changing American Character* (New Haven, CT: Yale University Press, 1950), David M. Potter, *People of Plenty: Economic Abundance and the American Character* (Chicago: University of Chicago Press, 1954), Daniel Bell, *The End of Ideology: On the Exhaustion of Political Ideas in the Fifties* (Glencoe, IL: Free Press, 1960), and Eric F. Goldman, *The Crucial Decade—And After: America, 1945–1960* (New York: Vintage Books, 1960).

4. For a concise tour of the earliest days, see John M. Murrin, "Religion and Politics in America from the First Settlements to the Civil War," Chapter 1 in Mark A. Noll and Luke E. Harlow, eds., *Religion and American Politics: From the Colonial Period to the Present* (New York: Oxford University Press, 1990). On the first "great awakening" and its political associations, see Daniel Walker Howe, *What Hath God Wrought: The Transformation of America, 1815–1848* (Oxford: Oxford University Press, 2007).

5. Paul Kleppner, *The Cross of Culture: A Social Analysis of Midwestern Politics, 1850–1900* (New York: Free Press, 1970), and Richard J. Jensen, *The Winning of the Midwest: Social and Political Conflict, 1888–1896* (Chicago: University of Chicago Press, 1971). See also Thomas R. Pegram, *Battling Demon Rum: The Struggle for a Dry America, 1800–1933* (Chicago: Ivan Dee, 1998).

NOTES   167

6. For major religious families at the time, see Will Herberg, *Protestant, Catholic, Jew: An Essay in American Religious Sociology* (Garden City, NY: Doubleday, 1960). See also Lyman Kellstedt, John Green, Corwin Smidt, and James Guth, "Faith Transformed: Religion and American Politics from FDR to George W. Bush," Chapter 12 in Noll and Harlow, eds., *Religion and American Politics*.

7. Seymour Martin Lipset echoes and extends Edmund Burke on the United States as "the Protestants of Protestantism, the Dissenters of Dissent," in Lipset, *American Exceptionalism: A Double-Edged Sword* (New York: W. W. Norton, 1996), 60–62. For the nature of religious distinctions within Protestantism, see Robert P. Swierenga, "The Liturgical-Pietist Continuum," 150–153, in Noll and Harlow, *Religion and American Politics*.

8. For arguments that this was more than metaphorical, see C. Wright Mills, *The Power Elite* (New York: Oxford University Press, 1956), and E. Digby Baltzell, *The Protestant Establishment* (New York: Random House, 1964).

9. James S. Hennesey, *American Catholic: A History of the Roman Catholic Community in the United States* (New York: Oxford University Press, 1981), and Jay P. Dolan, *The American Catholic Experience: A History from Colonial Times to the Present* (Garden City, NY: Doubleday, 1985).

10. The religious family that *was* ideologically distinctive was the Others, well left of center on cultural concerns but by far the smallest of the four. Jewish Americans were still central to this aggregate of Others in this first postwar period, though they would become far less so as time passed. Lawrence H. Fuchs, *The Political Behavior of American Jews* (Glencoe, IL: Free Press, 1956), and Kenneth D. Wald, *The Foundations of American Jewish Liberalism* (Cambridge: Cambridge University Press, 2019).

11. Charles R. Wilson and Mark Silk, eds., *Religion and Public Life in the South: In the Evangelical Mode* (Walnut Creek, CA: Alta Mira Press, 2005).

12. This is not to say that Protestant Evangelicals, who were ultimately key to triggering a new partisan mobilization, had not been developing organized political intermediaries of their own before the partisan explosion to come, only that these intermediaries were not initially integral to the active parties. See Ralph Chandler Clark, "The Wicked Shall Not Bear Rule: The Fundamentalist Heritage of the New Christian Right," in David G. Bromley and Anson Shupe, eds., *New Christian Politics* (Macon, GA: Mercer University Press, 1984); Clyde Wilcox, *God's Warriors: The Christian Right in Twentieth Century America* (Baltimore: Johns Hopkins University Press, 1992); Matthew C. Moen, *The Transformation of the Christian Right* (Tuscaloosa: University of Alabama Press, 1992).

13. A systematic introduction to thinking about such developments is Geoffrey C. Layman, *The Great Divide: Religious and Cultural Conflict in American Party Politics* (New York: Columbia University Press, 2001). In a more applied fashion, see Layman, "Religions and Political Behavior in the United States: The Impact of Beliefs, Affiliations, and Commitment from 1980 to 1994," *Public Opinion Quarterly* 61(1997), 288–316.

14. These Others had also changed the most in their internal composition, being principally Jewish identifiers in the first postwar period but clustering among those who chose the religious option of "none" by the third era. The most regular and systematic registry of their evolution is probably the ongoing reportage from the Pew Research Center on Religion and Public Life (religionnewsletter@pewresearch.org).

15. This way of thinking might be traced to Herbert McClosky, Paul Hoffman, and Rosemary O'Hara, "Issue Conflict and Consensus among Party Leaders and Followers," *American Political Science Review* 54(1960), 406–427; McClosky, "Consensus and Ideology in American Politics," *American Political Science Review* 58(1964), 361–382; and Samuel Stouffer, *Communism, Conformity, and Civil Liberties* (New York: Doubleday, 1966). It was much more fully developed in McClosky and Dennis Chong, "Social Learning and the Acquisition of Political Norms," Chapter 8 in McClosky and John Zaller, *The American Ethos: Public Attitudes toward Capitalism and Democracy* (Cambridge, MA: Harvard University Press, 1984).

16. Indeed, the more extreme among them provided further goads to the political awakening among Evangelical Protestants. Leading this deliberate incitement of a conservative response was that self-conscious "counter-culture": Todd Gitlin, *The Sixties: Years of Hope, Days of Rage* (New York: Bantam, 1993). One prologue was anti-war protest during the Vietnam War: Charles DeBenedetti, *An American Ordeal: The Antiwar Movement of the Vietnam Era*

(Syracuse, NY: Syracuse University Press, 1990). For the long battle inside the Democratic Party to counteract these effects, see Kenneth S. Baer, *Reinventing Democrats: The Politics of Liberalism from Clinton to Reagan* (Lawrence: University Press of Kansas, 2000).

17. A sense of the "raw material" available for this new construction, that is, the array of items tapping cultural politics along with public preferences on them, can be gained from three works appearing at roughly the beginning of the modern postwar era: Benjamin L. Page and Robert Y. Shapiro, *The Rational Public: Fifty Years of Trends in American Policy Preferences* (Chicago: University of Chicago Press, 1991); Samuel L. Popkin, *The Reasoning Voter: Communication and Persuasion in Presidential Campaigns* (Chicago: University of Chicago Press, 1991); and William G. Mayer, *The Changing American Mind: How and Why American Public Opinion Changed between 1960 and 1988* (Ann Arbor: University of Michigan Press, 1992).

18. Even analysts who saw incipient change on cultural values within Republican ranks were not likely to parse it additionally by internal party structure. One exception is John C. Green, James L. Guth, and Cleveland R. Fraser, "Apostles and Apostates? Religion and Politics among Party Activists," in Green and Guth, eds., *The Bible and the Ballot Box: Religion and Politics in the 1988 Elections* (Boulder, CO: Westview, 1981). More generally, see Lyman A. Kellstedt and John C. Green, "Knowing God's Many People: Denominational Preference and Political Behavior," in David Leege and Kellstedt, eds., *Rediscovering the Religious Factor in American Politics* (Armonk, NY: M. E. Sharpe, 1993).

19. Though note that in this third era, despite a major conservative move by Republican activists, the representational gap on cultural values—that is, the distance between activists and their rank and file in each party—remained much larger among Democrats than among Republicans.

20. Change on this scale, even as it represented a clear gain for the Republican Party, was unlikely to occur without major attendant tensions, and in fact it did not. Duane Murray Oldfield, *The Right and the Righteous: The Christian Right Confronts the Republican Party* (Lanham, MD: Rowman & Littlefield, 1996); Kimberly H. Conger, *The Christian Right in Republican State Politics* (New York: Palgrave, 2009).

21. Denominational Others in the South had already shown substantial partisan distance in the preceding period, though Republican Others had been a tiny population at that point.

22. For an example attending to class, race, and religion for their relationship to political behavior in the dissident region, the South, see Byron E. Shafer and Richard Johnston, "Partisan Change in the Post-Key South," Chapter 8 in Angie Maxwell and Todd G. Shields, eds., *Unlocking V.O. Key, Jr.: "Southern Politics" for the Twenty-First Century* (Fayetteville: University of Arkansas Press, 2012).

23. For another approach, which parallels ours, see the standard text from Kenneth D. Wald and Allison Calhoun-Brown, *Religion and Politics in the United States*, 8th ed. (Lanham, MD: Rowman & Littlefield, 2018).

24. Among many, Robert Fowler, Allen Hertzke, Laura Olson, and Kevin Den Dulk argue for this further denominational distinction in their widely used overview of religion and politics in the United States: Fowler, Hertzke, Olson, and Den Dulk, *Religion and Politics in America*, 8th ed. (Philadelphia: Routledge, 2018). Geoffrey Layman does the same: see Table 2.1 in Layman, *The Great Divide*, 72–73.

25. The theoretically desirable test of the two approaches is to demonstrate that black Evangelicals differ from black non-Evangelicals in their cultural preferences, guaranteeing that black Evangelicalism is not just an indirect measure of racial background. But empirically, the overwhelming choice of Evangelical Protestantism by black Americans makes a test measure—policy preferences among black non-Evangelicals—unreliable.

26. Among individuals, see Richard Allen, Michael J. Dawson, and Ronald Brown, "Racial Belief Systems, Religious Guidance, and African-American Political Participation," *National Political Science Review* 2(1990), 22–44; among institutions, see C. Eric Lincoln and Lawrence H. Mamiya, *The Black Church in the African-American Experience* (Durham, NC: Duke University Press, 1990).

27. Though even here there was a regional overlay, in that black Evangelicals were modestly conservative and not liberal at all in the South (at +.03) (table not shown).

NOTES 169

28. The term was popularized in James Davison Hunter, *Culture Wars: The Struggle to Define America* (New York: Basic, 1991), followed by Hunter, *Before the Shooting Begins: Searching for Democracy in America's Culture Wars* (New York: Macmillan, 1994).

29. See note 3 for landmarks of the time.

30. This approach accords more with efforts to put these changes together in a less apocalyptic fashion as with John C. Green, James L. Guth, Corwin E. Smidt, and Lyman A. Kellstedt, *Religion and the Culture Wars* (Lanham, MD: Rowman & Littlefield, 1996). More pointedly, Geoffrey C. Layman and John C. Green, "Wars and Rumors of Wars: The Contexts of Cultural Conflict in American Political Behavior," *British Journal of Political Science* 36(2006), 61–89.

31. David O. Moberg, *The Great Reversal: Evangelicalism versus Social Concern* (Philadelphia: Lippincott, 1974).

32. What would likely not have been recognized in its time was that another theoretical notion about the political implications of American religious society had simultaneously been laid to rest. This was the notion of the United States as a "Protestant nation." That view was alive and well in the immediate postwar years, surviving comfortably into the successor period. But the partisan mobilization that began in this second period and exploded in the third would be fatal to its argument, for as cultural issues gained partisan traction in American politics, the two great Protestant families were moving in opposite ideological directions.

Chapter 4

1. These are the four great social cleavages used by Jeff Manza and Clem Brooks in a related earlier work, Manza and Brooks, *Social Cleavages and Political Change: Voter Alignments and U.S. Party Coalitions* (New York: Oxford University Press, 1999), where their Chapter 5, on "Gender," is an especially rich tour of the alternative ways in which this cleavage has been treated.

2. An argument that this is indeed the inescapable fourth of the four major policy conflicts that have characterized American politics since the Great Depression is William J. M. Claggett and Byron E. Shafer, *The American Public Mind: The Issue Structure of Mass Politics in the Postwar United States* (Cambridge: Cambridge University Press, 2010), especially Part I, "The Structure of Public Preferences," which was the original source of the measures extended and used here.

3. An early attempt to put some empirical data behind these initial postwar impressions is Tom Smith, "The Polls: Gender and Attitudes toward Violence," *Public Opinion Quarterly* 48(1984), 384–396. The main alternative was a vague and general expectation that women should be more conservative than men, though a closer look at this work suggests that it is in effect focused on a generalized conservatism—what we might call "cultural traditionalism"—more than on any specific policy domain. For example, see Bernard Berelson and Paul Lazarsfeld, "Women: A Major Problem for the P.A.C.," *Public Opinion Quarterly* 9(1945), 79–82.

4. For the comprehensive narrative, see John Lewis Gaddes, *The Cold War* (London: Penguin, 2007).

5. "Politics stops at the water's edge" was the argument of Senator Arthur Vandenberg in support of what became known as the Vandenberg Resolution (S. Res. 23), a keystone in the creation of major national security institutions as the Cold War heated up.

6. In these opening years, there was also an implicit expectation in some related literature about the role of sex with regard to civil rights, to the effect that women, being more removed from arguments about appropriate rules and procedures for civic life, would be less concerned with adjusting them. This shows up, for example, in Samuel Stouffer, *Communism, Conformity, and Civil Liberties* (Garden City, NY: Doubleday, 1955), 131–149.

7. The expectation that women would reflect an overall cultural conservatism in American society more automatically than men was also readily available as grounds for a hypothesized theoretical difference by sex on policy preferences in the domain of cultural values, as in Seymour Martin Lipset, *Political Man: The Social Bases of Politics* (Garden City, NY: Doubleday, 1960), 216–217.

8. There would be a retrospective argument that social welfare should provide a consistent and ongoing contribution by sex to partisan alignments, whereby women were expected to lean liberal and men conservative. Early results ran in that direction but were quite modest, as with

170 NOTES

Robert Shapiro and Harpreet Mahajan, "Gender Differences in Policy Preferences," *Public Opinion* 50(1986), 42–61.

9. The standard work for approaching Southern culture as a general phenomenon in the years before there was serious survey data was W. J. Cash, *The Mind of the South* (New York: Knopf, 1941), just as the standard work for approaching Southern politics within that culture was V. O. Key Jr., *Southern Politics in State and Nation* (New York: Knopf, 1949).

10. A third way to interpret these extremely discordant results for national security is to allow the two regions to align their parties on what are effectively two substantively different dimensions. For the North, liberals were the doves in a Cold War, while Republicans were the harks. But for the South, liberals were the internationalists, and conservatives were the isolationists. That posits national security as the domain that did not have even a nationally generalized interpretation in these early postwar years. Results for national security in subsequent eras will add reinforcement to this view.

11. In terms of theoretical expectations, "Southern womanhood" played an important role for Southern men and not just Southern women in Cash, *The Mind of the South.*

12. Robert A. Divine, *The Illusion of Neutrality* (Chicago: University of Chicago Press, 1962); John Lewis Gaddis, *The United States and the Origins of the Cold War* (New York: Columbia University Press, 1926).

13. Alonzo L. Hamby, *The Imperial Years: The United States since 1939* (New York: Weybright and Talley, 1976); Charles DeBenedetti, *An American Ordeal: The Antiwar Movement of the Vietnam Era* (Syracuse, NY: Syracuse University Press, 1990).

14. In the aftermath of this increase, there would be a retrospective argument that sex *should* provide a consistent and ongoing contribution to partisan alignments on social welfare, with women leaning liberal and men conservative. Systematic results in that direction were available in this second postwar period, though these results were quite modest, as with Robert Shapiro and Harpreet Mahajan, "Gender Differences in Policy Preferences," *Public Opinion* 50(1986), 42–61.

15. Southern Democratic women made the largest individual move, coming from just left of the national average to a solidly liberal position and punctuating the end of the region as a shaping influence on partisan alignments when they did so.

16. These distinctions are often approached through the notion of an electoral gap, the difference between male and female vote choice, rather than through party attachment. A thorough introduction to the gap as conventionally defined, including alternative definitions and alternative theories for the rise and evolution of the phenomenon, is Jeff Manza and Clem Brooks, "The Gender Gap in U.S. Presidential Elections: When? Why? Implications?," *American Journal of Sociology* 103(1998), 1235–1266. A historical precursor to analyses of the gap as defined by vote choice rather than party attachment is Malcolm M. Willey and Stuart A. Rice, "A Sex Cleavage in the Presidential Election of 1920," *Journal of the American Statistical Association* 19(1924), 519–520.

17. More recent work along the same lines has started to look at race, education, and income differences among women, treating women (and implicitly men) less like potentially homogenous blocs. See Erin C. Cassese and Tiffany D. Barnes, "Reconciling Sexism and Women's Support for Republican Candidates: A Look at Gender, Class, and Whiteness in the 2012 and 2016 Presidential Races," *Political Behavior* 41(2019), 677–700.

18. Some existing research has gone in search of a specific but larger societal contribution to this overall evolution, as with Janet Box-Steffensmeier, Suzanna De Boef, and Tse-Min Lin, "The Dynamics of the Partisan Gender Gap," *American Political Science Review* 98(2004), 515–528, suggesting that the growing gender divide was in part driven by women's reaction to societal conditions, such as a growing conservatism of the political climate or an increase in the number of economically vulnerable single women.

19. There is some recent work that suggests that a partisan gender gap might in part have been a product of early and deliberate efforts by left-of-center activists to cooperate extensively with progressive women's organizations, as in Silvia Erzeel and Karen Celis, "Political Parties, Ideology, and the Substantive Representation of Women," *Party Politics* 22(2015), 576–586.

NOTES 171

20. Activists tend to be more ideologically extreme (Nathaniel A. Birkhead and Marjorie Random Hershey, "Assessing the Ideological Extremism of American Party Activists," *Party Politics* 25[2019], 495–506), more programatically consistent (John R. Zaller, *The Nature and Origins of Mass Opinion* [Cambridge: Cambridge University Press, 1992]), and more motivated by ideological and issue-based goals and concerns (Edmond Costantini and Linda O. Valenty, "The Motives-Ideology Connection among Political Party Activists," *Political Psychology* 17[1996], 497–524), all of which create higher barriers for partisan realignment.

21. An interesting echo of the same analytic tension can be found in an entirely different realm by way of Annette Bernhardt, Martina Morris, and Mark Hancock, "Women's Gains, Men's Losses? The Shrinking Gender Gap in Earnings," *American Journal of Sociology* 101(1995), 302–328.

22. This also reflects previous findings on sex and partisanship highlighting the comparative ideological moderation of Republican women, as with Tiffany D. Barnes and Erin C. Cassese, "American Party Women: A Look at the Gender Gap within Parties," *Political Research Quarterly* 70(2017), 127–141, which finds Republican women to be considerably left of their male co-partisans on the scope of government and responses to inequality. Similar results have been found in the British context, where conservative women have likewise been found to the left of their male co-partisans, but only on specifically economic issues (Rosie Campbell and Sarah Childs, "To the Left, to the Right: Representing Conservative Women's Interests," *Party Politics* 21(2015), 626–637).

Conclusion

1. For the New Deal and the welfare state, see Anthony J. Badger, *The New Deal: The Depression Years, 1933–1940* (Chicago: Ivan R. Dee, 2002). For the initial discovery of this partisan alignment, see Angus Campbell, Philip E. Converse, Warren E. Mille, and Donald E. Stokes, *The American Voter* (New York: Wiley, 1960).

2. For the New Deal and civil rights, see James T. Patterson, *Congressional Conservatism and the New Deal* (Lexington: University Press of Kentucky, 1967). For the evolution of the rights domain, see Richard M. Valelly, *The Two Reconstructions: The Struggle for Black Enfranchisement* (Chicago: University of Chicago, 2004).

3. For national security in the opening postwar years, see John Lewis Gaddis, *The United States and the Origins of the Cold War, 1941–1947* (New York: Columbia University Press, 1972). For the ideological disarray around issues of national security, see Wayne S. Cole, *Roosevelt and the Isolationists, 1932–1945* (Lincoln: University of Nebraska Press, 1983).

4. For a comprehensive way to approach cultural values and party politics, see Geoffrey C. Layman, *Religious and Cultural Conflict in American Party Politics* (New York: Columbia University Press, 2001). For those conflicts in an earlier—and more intense—era, see Paul Kleppner, *The Cross of Culture: A Social Analysis of Midwestern Politics, 1850–1900* (New York: Free Press, 1970).

5. The Democratic gap of .08 in Table C.2.A is the difference between the mean Democratic position on social welfare (−.16 in Table C.1.A) and the mean Democratic score on civil rights (−.08 in Table C.1.B). The Republican gap of .12 in Table C.2.A is likewise the difference between the mean Republican position on social welfare- (+.24 in Table C.1.A) and the mean Republican score on civil rights (+.12 in Table C.1.B). The total gap merely sums those scores (.08 + .12).

6. Among many, see Eric M. Patashnik and Wendy J. Schiller, eds., *Dynamics of American Democracy: Partisan Polarization, Political Competition, and Government Performance* (Lawrence: University Press of Kansas, 2020), and Sam Rosenfeld, *The Polarizers: Postwar Architects of Our Partisan Era* (Chicago: University of Chicago Press, 2017).

7. Among many, see Charles M. Price and Joseph Boskin, "The Roosevelt 'Purge': A Reappraisal," *Journal of Politics* 28(1966), 660–670.

8. Recall that the black Evangelicals contained effectively no Republicans, making partisan mobilization irrelevant to them.

Afterword

1. Even then, the smallest of these regional party samples already generate two modestly anomalous results. Figure A.4 is not constructed to accommodate negative relationships, but there were two tiny versions among Southern Republicans, for national security in the first postwar period and cultural values in the second, whereby rank-and-file members who were more *conservative* than their own activists defected to the other party. The substantive point here is that both were effectively −.00, that is, nonrelationships with respect to the voting analysis. Nevertheless, those numbers are missing from the Southern Republican panels in Era 1 and Era 2 respectively in Figure A.4.

INDEX

American National Election Study (ANES), 10

black Evangelicalism and cultural values, 82–83

civil rights, as a policy domain, 3, 40–41
   and geographic region, 44–45, 53–56
   marker items, 154–155
   and party attachment, 40–41
   and racial background with party attachment,
     123–124
   and racialized factions, 41–42
   rights preferences and racial background, 42
   and welfare preference, 42
Civil Rights Act of 1964, 47
comparative priorities and voting behavior,
   139–144
cultural values, as a policy domain, 3, 66–67
   and denominational membership, 68–69,
     72–73
   with denominational membership and party
     attachment, 125–126
   and geographic region, 77, 79
   marker items, 156–157
   and party attachment, 68, 72
culture wars, 84–85

denominational membership, as a social cleavage, 3
   and cultural values by geographic region, 77–80
   over time, 84
   and party attachment, 67
   as a share of American society, 67, 74
   as a share of geographic regions, 69–70, 77

Evangelical Protestantism by race, 81

geographic region, as a social cleavage, 4
   and policy preferences by party, 93

isolationism, 13

national security, as a policy domain, 3, 89
   marker items, 155–156
   and party attachment, 13, 99
   and social class, 13
New Deal, 9–10
normalcy, 66

partisan alignment by geographic region, 118–119
partisan alignments, defined, 2–3
   by geographic region, 118–119
   by policy domain, 113–114
   and political change, 39–40
   by sex, 95–96
partisan balance, as a change process, 5, 107–110
partisan convergence, across policy domains,
   112–116
partisan intermediation, as a change process, 5,
   33–38
   and welfare preferences, 10–16, 22
partisan mobilization, as a change process, 5, 66,
   84–88
party activists, defined, 3–4
   and cultural values, 75
   and rights preferences, 43, 52–53, 57–60
   and social class, 14–15, 24–25
party attachments, defined, 2
party rank and files, defined, 3–4
   and cultural values, 75–76
   and rights preferences, 43, 52–53, 57–60
   by sex, 105–106
   and social class, 14–15, 24–25
policy preferences, defined, 2, 11
   by party, 76
   and sex, 91, 97
political parties, by sex, 103

racialized factions and rights preferences by
   region, 45, 53–56
   and partisan change, 48–51

173

sex, defined, 3
  and partisan balance, 90, 101–102
  and party attachment, 91
  by party, sex, and region, 100–101
  policy preferences by sex and region, 93
  as a social cleavage, 89
social class, as a social cleavage, 2
  and party attachment, 12, 22–23
social cleavages, defined, 2
  and partisan alignment, 121–128
social roots of political conflict, 128–135
social welfare, defined, 3
  marker items, 154
  as a policy domain, 9, 38
Southern politics, 18, 29–31

welfare preferences and social class, 16–17, 27–28
  and geographic region, 16–17, 27–28
  and party attachment, 16–17, 27–28
  and party structure, 19–21, 28–29, 31–32
  and rights preferences by region, 46
  and social class and party attachment, 122–123

voter enfranchisement as a change process, 5, 47–53, 60–64
voting behavior and geographic region, 144–150
Voting Rights Act of 1965, 47